THIS AUGUST

Coming Out of the Blind Spot

A Memoir of Hope

Kimberly D. Benn

All scripture quotations marked KJV are taken from *The Holy Bible*, King James Version, Thomas Nelson 1984

All scripture quotations marked NIV are taken from *The Holy Bible*, New International Version, Zondervan 2005

Cover Design — Jo of Smoot Aesthetic
Interior Design – B.O.Y. Enterprises, Inc.

ISBN-13: 978-0-578-40917-7
ISBN-10: 0578409178

Printed in the United States of America.

DEDICATION

This book is dedicated to my sweetest blessing, Kayla. You
have given Mommy a million reasons to live purposefully
and without regret. Because of you, Mommy is emerging
completely from the blind spot. You are the wind beneath
my wings, and the reason I have changed the narrative of
our lives. I love you!

ACKNOWLEDGEMENTS

Special thanks to my family for continuing to push me to be my best authentic self, encouraging me to follow every dream, and cheering me on when I felt like cowering in the nearest corner. Daddy (Thomas) and Ma (Mary), you have been my greatest teachers and motivators. Your demonstrations of accountability and strength have fueled and guided me. Great thanks to my eldest brother David, for introducing me to many of my "firsts" while tirelessly pressing me to finish what I start. Because of you, I have made "finishing" my life's mantra. Big thanks to my brother, Allan "aka" Jeff for always having my back! Big thanks to my Aunt Arlene Benn-Bozeman, your soul-filled advice has steeped healing into my thoughts in the aftermath of divorce and emotional breakdown. We are better because of you!

To the greatest builder of people, my Spiritual Father and forever pastor Carlton C. Spruill, Sr. —your wisdom, guidance, and ministry have changed the trajectory of my life. Thank you for preaching the life-changing Word, for loving and guiding me through a transition filled with uncharted waters and reminding me that "I can survive the transition!" To my spiritual mother, Ira M. Coleman—thank you for loving me through rejection to repair. The deliverance ministry birthed in you is the vehicle that ushers in the Ruach breath of God. To my brother, Pastor Elijah Goodwin, Jr., thank you for the love and support demonstrated through the years and for always believing in me. Big love to my sister-friend Renee Boston, words cannot express the love and gratitude your presence brings to my life. I need you to survive.

Great thanks to my Spiritual T.A.L.K. sisters, Tanisha "Nikki" Robinson, Ayana George, and LaMika "my day one" Hughes,—your constant love, prayers, support, sisterhood, and visibility have defined friendship and sisterhood for me. Yemi O. Fawehinmi, my "ear to the street" - thank you for always asking the hard questions and challenging me to be better. Tawanda-Nicole, my sister, thank you for always supporting and lending your ear, I love you! Tanya Higgins Russell, thanks for the gift of friendship, giving the best advice, and being the shoulder, I needed to cry on when I was searching for answers. Tiffany A. Jackson, thank you for every prayer, encouraging word, and years of support. Your faith is contagious. Much love to Monique Brown, thank you for silently supporting me through the years.   JoVanni Smoot, thank you for lending your creative genius to this project, the cover is bad to the bone.

I thank my North Carolina villagers, Sharon Monroe and Quanetta Crawley, for holding my hand and always allowing me to be myself in a judgment-free zone. We are moving forward - mind, body, and spirit! Alana Weaver Bennett and Tamma L. Simpson, thank you for pushing me to walk out my ministry and holding me to task. Finally, to my Naomi's Posture: Women in Transition sisters, you are an enormous blessing and we continue to stand strong in the posture of victory!

FOREWORD

This amazing narrative sheds light upon the Grace of God in our lives. Grace is the amazing favor of God in our ever-changing lives as we pursue our destiny. *Coming Out of the Blind Spot* is a literary demonstration of God's love for His people. In the fullness of His deity, God manifests His love for our challenged humanity and makes Grace go where it does not belong. God's Grace is amazing.

Coming Out of The Blind Spot is a powerful autobiographical memoir that traces a journey with God through the sometimes-painful requirements of life to reach maturity and destiny. This carefully-crafted narrative reveals God's involvement and His careful management of our lives. God's Grace is clearly revealed as the memoir provides testimony of the human struggle and the providence of God in care of our purpose. Each experience of life is clearly shown to be a building block of character and of glory to God. Each chapter shows the impact of the testimony of life, and highlights God's involvement in our story. This book is difficult to put down. It is powerful and passionate.

The lessons of each narrative truth provide wonderful

strategies for the resolution of life's unexpected experiences. *Coming Out of the Blind Spot* underscores the importance of understanding our heritage and our histories. The real experiences of life impact our future reality, and the hope of the narrative drives the reader to envision a promising future that includes all that we are yet becoming. The truthful testimonies help us to see God in all things, as the evolution of love is clear and empowered by our choices, both right and wrong. God and His love are clearly present throughout the memoir, and the omnipresence of God fills the testimonies of life in real-time.

It is certain that human fragility is a common challenge for each of us. The exposure of the fragility and complexity of human relationships points us to our need for God, even as we remain in His love. *Coming Out of the Blind Spot* is a brave evangelistic narrative that directs us to the God who we know can handle all things. Sometimes it not safe to be human, but a message of hope moves through the pages of the narrative and uncovers the divine involvement of God, raising the importance of faith in our life lives. As the scriptures remind us, it is certain that without faith it is impossible to please God.

The redemptive work of God emerges from the pages as the narrative leads us out of the blind spots of life. The deceptive possibilities of life are endless, but they are trumped by God's love and His Grace. *To God Be the Glory*.

This is a wonderful read, and you will find the narrative balanced, theistically sound, and secure in biblical truth. The narrative is truly human, highlighting inspiration in such a way that moves the reader to a place of deliverance by faith. It is certain that no matter the path our lives take, God will be faithful, and will lead us out. Enjoy this read, and *come out of the blind spot*.

Pastor Carlton C. Spruill

Table of Contents

Prayer

Most Holy God, we bless Your Name and honor You. We make Your Name great, and we call upon your Holy Ghost power to renew the mind of the reader. In the name of Jesus, we come before You ready for an emotional cleansing. We pray that each broken person who holds this book, finds their way back to you for a supernatural healing that will alter the very fabric of their lives. God, we believe that by the time the reader reaches the last page of this book, they will know how and why you created them, embrace the grace that brought them to this moment, and allow Your Word to usher them to a place of eternal Truth and divine acceptance. Lord, we thank You for each reader, each merchant, and each person who has sown this book as a seed into a woman's life. We ask that You would meet every emotional need.

Thank You for the blessings of grace and mercy that You consistently give to us, even when we feel as though You have abandoned us. We are not what we have been through, what we have become, or what has happened to us. Thank You for the grace to conquer every mountain that we face, and the strength to fight through each low place into which we may fall. Though the enemy formed weapons in our past that were meant for our destruction, they did not prosper because You have armed us with spiritual weapons to fight a good warfare! We declare victory in Jesus' Name.

For each woman who has felt weak, lost, alone, rejected, manipulated, or preyed upon, we ask that you would blow Your Ruach life-giving breath, on her today. We speak a healing and life to each broken and shamed part of her, in the Name of Jesus. We lift up every woman and man who has been victimized, overlooked, mishandled, penetrated, violated, raped, molested, fondled, groped, or sodomized. We curse the residue left behind from the abuse, and we command the spirit of shame and perversion to uprooted, and every unholy soul tie to be broken, in Jesus' Name. God, we ask that You enter the bowels of every broken woman to find the imprisoned little girl and release her from the bondage and shame she carries. We believe that by the time she has finished reading this book and has called upon Your Name, the scales will be removed from her eyes, and she will begin to embrace the life that You have created for her. We know that nothing just *happens*—each bump in the road was set in place to make her better and to show the little girl within her that she was born to win. We Thank you for each step and each stop that allowed to her to be here.

Lord, please provide the strength to conquer every dysfunctional circumstance and memory of the past. Give us the fortitude to walk out our deliverance in spite of our dark past. Grant us the determination to press on to healthy places, no matter how tempting slipping backward may appear.

God, purge us with hyssop, and we shall be clean; wash us, and we will be whiter than snow. We receive freedom, liberty, and the victorious life that we have in You. In Jesus' Name we pray. Amen.

Introduction

This August Coming Out of the Blind Spot is about a woman who reached back to embrace and heal her younger-self and give a voice to an unspoken pattern that influenced her life. While on the journey to healing and wholeness she discovered an uncommunicable roadmap, which influenced many of her decisions and behaviors. Life and time have a way of moving you along but movement does not always equate to advancing. This August outlines the complexities of human relationship and the sovereignty of God navigating our lives. The events shared in this book are inspired by real life experiences, and not intended to hurt anyone. The truth revealed in this memoire exposes a cultivated and learned behavior which lead to a dysfunction that could only be addressed through self-work, prayer and fellowship with God the Father. The expectation for the reader is to begin their healing and deliverance and rent the garments of their shame which shroud their silent suffering.

THIS AUGUST

Coming Out of the Blind Spot

Acts 27:39–44

³⁹ When daylight came, they did not recognize the land, but they saw a bay with a sandy beach, where they decided to run the ship aground if they could. ⁴⁰ Cutting loose the anchors, they left them in the sea and at the same time untied the ropes that held the rudders. Then they hoisted the foresail to the wind and made for the beach. ⁴¹ But the ship struck a sandbar and ran aground. The bow stuck fast and would not move, and the stern was broken to pieces by the pounding of the surf. ⁴² The soldiers planned to kill the prisoners to prevent any of them from swimming away and escaping. ⁴³ But the centurion wanted to spare Paul's life and kept them from

carrying out their plan. He ordered those who could swim to jump overboard first and get to land. [44] The rest were to get there on planks or on other pieces of the ship. In this way everyone reached land safely.

Have You Considered the Season?

At the tender age of 19, I was invited to a prayer meeting and fellowship at Evangelist Reid's house. She and I sang together in a local community choir, and we had grown up within the same church fellowship. As I entered the apartment, I felt shy and reserved. I felt like a grasshopper among spiritual giants as she introduced me to the men and women in the room. At the prayer, I met a petite woman with a quirky and mysterious, yet grandiose personality. She was bold and no-nonsense; boldly declaring her confidence in the Jesus she served. This woman meant business! She firmly believed that what she said mattered to God. And if she gave you a prophetic word, you could trust it. I had never met anyone like this woman before. I was both afraid and intrigued by her. She looked like any other woman, but she was far from average. At 4 feet 11 inches, she was short of stature, but she was a giant in the spiritual realm!

Through her commitment to prayer and intercession on my behalf, this woman has made a significant impact on my life. Over the years, she has demonstrated her integrity as a woman of God who consistently reflects Christ. While this woman did not give birth to me naturally, she birthed me spiritually, and affectionately calls me her "daughter." We share life experiences with one another the ups and downs of ministry, the woes and wonders of family life, our relationships, career strides, and the mishaps our entrepreneurial endeavors. She listens carefully, but she rarely offers opinions or advice but simply encourages me to reflect Christ and agrees with me in prayer for God's divine direction. Instead of judgment for bad decisions, I received compassionate support and the tools to make fruitful decisions.

"Have you considered which season of life you're walking in?" This question that my spiritual mother gently challenged me to consider after a series of events continued to arise. Because of her influence, I have a better understanding of the seasons of life. Today, I issue you the same challenge: Have you considered the season that you are walking in?

Life seasons are different from the four seasons of the year. The four seasons of the year are timed and filled with a level of predictability. You can review a calendar to monitor when one season begins and the other ends, you can also check your surroundings and see flowers blooming, the trees' leaves changing colors or walk outside and see the vapors of your breath disappearing in the frigid air. Life seasons, on the contrary, are unpredictable, unscheduled, unscripted and can be filled with almost anything. In a life season every part of you and everything attached to you is experiencing the same thing simultaneously. Life seasons are not singular events, instead they are concurrent days, months or years of a singular type of event.

August is the eighth month and the beginning of the

third quarter in the calendar year. It's the fifth of the seven months that have 31 days, and it represents the waning of Summer and the onset of Fall. For me, August was the first month of the season shift, and the following months were filled with rejection and chaos. August represents the beginning of a hostile season which led to a lonely and cold Fall.

To every thing there is a season, and a time to every purpose under the heaven: [2]A time to be born, and a time to die; a time to plant, and a time to pluck up that which is planted; [3]A time to kill, and a time to heal; a time to break down, and a time to build up; [4]A time to weep, and a time to laugh; a time to mourn, and a time to dance; [5]A time to cast away stones, and a time to gather stones together; a time to embrace, and a time to refrain from embracing; [6]A time to get, and a time to lose; a time to keep, and a time to cast away; [7]A time to rend, and a time to sew; a time to keep silence, and a time to speak; [8]A time to love, and a time to hate; a time of war, and a time of peace.

—Ecclesiastes 3: 1–8 (KJV)

Seasons + Interruptions **= TRANSITION**

This August season was a time of truth, dare, and consequences. One day, I woke up and realized that my August season was upon me again, and that it caught me unaware. There was no call ahead for this 3AM reservation; it didn't send up a smoke signal as a warning; there was no notice of pending destruction—it just showed up with a devastating boom and crashed upon me like a wrecking ball. Countless casualties could be found amongst the debris, broken hearts, silent suffering, and painful memories. Something immense was about to explode and wreck my world which would reconcile my lofty expectations with my bleak reality. We want our lives to be stress-free, definitive, smooth-sailing, and without interruptions, but when truth prevails, life is often just the opposite. Each fork in the road, each impasse, each obstacle, and each pothole that slowly and irritatingly realigns the drive system is uncontrollably yet safely bringing you to your current moment. This journey of destruction and awakening is marred with lies and deceit, and couldn't possibly yield positive results for everyone involved—we can only be confident that God will be glorified.

IT HAD TO HAPPEN…

I found myself constantly asking God…

"Why is transition so prevalent in my life? Why is it a constant theme for me? Will the wheels of uncertainty ever rest their motion? Will there ever be peace—not the kind of peace that provokes questions about missing the rapture, but the peace of finding, knowing, and parking in a place that you confidently know is best, and where you can let out a big sigh of relief?"

I have often observed others laughing and navigating their seemingly perfect lives, and I have wondered if their lives were actively transitioning, or if they were better at managing and masking their transitions. These individuals don't appear stressed, and they seem to cope with their circumstances and coast along nicely without any visible conflict. Because they never utter a word about how life constantly serves them a litany of unexpectedly overwhelming blows and challenges, I often guess that because things "look" good, they must *be* good. It seemed like my life was constantly in transition—that I was always at the place where two seas meet and things become undone. Fortunately, this is not the story of my entire life, but only the part of my life related to romantic relationships—the area of my heart that I gave away with little regard for myself and with strong concern for the other person's needs, all while telling myself, *I'll work with what I'm getting,* even if what I was getting was garbage.

My spiritual father, Pastor Carlton C. Spruill, delivered a message one Sunday morning in 2005 that was titled "The Place Where Two Seas Meet." He confidently mounted the pulpit and read the text from Acts 27: 27–42. On that Sunday morning, it was as though only he and I were seated in the 1,000-seat cathedral, and I felt that he was speaking directly to me. Years before that moment, I couldn't conceive of divorcing my husband, even though I felt as though my life, which had been sailing along nicely, had suddenly hit an unseen and unexpected diversion that caused my life to become undone, forcing me to find a broken piece to float upon until I could reach safety and see clearly.

On that Sunday morning, Pastor Spruill gave an elegant exegesis of the text, and I was mesmerized by his skill as he delivered the poignant message. The anointing and revelation of God that I witnessed that day was palpable, and I could feel chains breaking from my life. He preached about the unseen working in the blind spots of your life that have the power to change or detour your life's course. Oh, I danced all over the church declaring victory through the storm and God's vision for a clearer life—I was confidently assured that I would survive the interruption!

DIARY ENTRY

Friday, January 23, 2015 - 10:21PM

This man knows how to get to you…

The year was 2002, and we sat in a circle while Pastor Spruill taught a class called the "Timothy Project." The class took place during the week, and many of us had come to the class after work, exhausted and yet making every effort to be present in the moment by answering questions and participating in the discussion. We had our notebooks and Bibles in hand, and some even had tape recorders. We were preparing ourselves for ministry, and the Pastor was imparting his knowledge and wisdom to us. The members of the class were Ministers, Ministers-in-Training, Deacons, and lay people from our church and other churches. You had to be invited to attend the class, and I couldn't help but wonder, *ummm… why was I invited here?* That night, my Pastor said to me, "Benn, don't expect your life to be perfect, with a house and a white picket fence. You're not ordinary—you're extraordinary—and you're going to have to pay for that anointing on your life." Perhaps he couldn't see that I was rolling my eyes behind the look of shock on my face, but I'm sure that my body language said it all, for in those two seconds, I felt that I had died and come back to life. I wanted to weep, slide off the chair onto the red carpet, and kick my feet—*I just want to be average! Pastor, I am so mad at you—why did you say that?* For many years after that moment, I replayed the scene in my mind. Perhaps some bumps in the road could have been avoided if I had not been trying to force a square peg to fit in a round hole all this time.

Temperatures

A thermostat senses the temperature of a system so that the system temperature is maintained near the desired set-point. A thermostat is often the main control unit of a heating or cooling system, and has applications ranging from ambient air control to automotive coolant control. Thermometers are also used in other applications such as electric clothing irons. It is a "closed loop" control device, as it seeks to reduce the error between the desired and measured temperatures. Sometimes, a thermostat combines both the sensing and control action elements of a controlled system, such as in an automotive thermostat.

I was raised in a loving two-parent home with my siblings. I'm the third of three children, educated in the Parochial and Roman Catholic school system from second grade through high school. I faithfully attended

Goodwill Baptist Church in the Bronx, where I was active in Sunday school and the church choir.

Both parents went to work daily. My mother was superwoman! She came home from work, she cooked dinner for the family, made sure the laundry was done and the floors were mopped, and kept the cabinets and closets filled with each household item in its respective place. My mother was a no-nonsense woman about her business. Although at times she didn't say much, when she spoke, you better listen. My mom was strong, caring and sassy. She taught you with her actions, demonstrated her love, and when trouble arose you could find her simultaneously bailing you out and fussing you out.

My father worked in the construction field during the week, and on the weekends, he had a second job as an entrepreneur and club owner. He was a sharp dresser and a sharp talker who was always talking about his business. He was a carpenter by trade, and there weren't many things that he couldn't do, fix, build, correct, or address. He was my hero, and if I asked him a question about anything, I was sure to find an answer. I recall that he would come home on the weekends and cover the glass-top dining room table with the thousands of dollars that he had made in the club the night before. Everyone who knew anyone partied at my dad's spot on the weekends, "Club 371" on Clay and Teller in the Bronx. I remember hearing horror stories of armed robbery attempts, and stories of partners disagreeing as they tried to calculate their share of the proceeds and control of the business. I also recall the fashion shows and the fun I experienced playing with the other partners' children. I remembered that everyone celebrated me as TJ's daughter. I would occasionally go to the club on Sunday afternoon to help my dad clean up after Saturday night, quickly eating a handful of the sweet cherries left behind the bar by the barmaid. I also remember collecting and cleaning the drinking glasses, playing billiards in the game room, and mounting the barstool to play the 25-cent slot machines and arcade games. I loved playing the slot machines and finding coins left in the sofas by the previous night's party-goers. I loved being with my Dad.

I can remember when things were volatile at home, but it appeared that in the course of a few days or a few hours, things would return back to "normal." My parents argued, as most adults did, and then Mom would make a hot meal as a sign of peace. Mom would cook thick slices of butcher's bacon or smothered pork chops with white rice and green beans, because those were Dad's favorite dishes. That's when I would know—the fight was over.

As I matured, I noticed my overwhelming tendency to find myself in the middle of the road when conflict presented itself. If the conflict was between others, I would be the one talking someone off the ledge and convincing them that confronting the issue wasn't worth the trouble. If the conflict was between family members, I didn't want to be a part of the triangular communication and refused to carry messages between the conflicting parties. Instead, I would convince both parties that the disagreement was beneath them, and that they should forget what happened and press forward. I learned how to unearth conflict but not engage in it, and I would stay on the perimeter of the disagreement. If I did engage in conflict, I masterfully stayed on the outskirts and refused to take sides—I knew how to be the thermometer or regulator of the conflict. I didn't want to hurt someone's feelings or make someone feel betrayed or isolated, and in my subconscious, I was keeping those involved in the conflict at bay. I practiced this dysfunctional yet non-confrontational behavior while serving in church, because I didn't want to ruffle feathers or rock the boat. Instead, I would go along to get along, even when my thoughts and opinions were solicited. I desperately wanted to be seen as a "nice" person, and my concerns of letting the cat out of bag were often unfounded, unsubstantiated, and baseless. Rather, I fabricated these excuses based on my own internal desire to avoid feeling disappointed, hurt, or anxious. My concern for how others could be hurt kept me tight-lipped with a false sense of peace. It was though I was saying to others, "if you like it, I love it, and I'm minding my business." The truth is that, while I appeared to be at peace with others,

I felt a sense of rage brewing internally, because I constantly ignored and discounted my own feelings. I replayed the same message to myself with each conflict, and I would dim my light and lower my voice while catering to others. Sadly, this only made me feel upset with those I wanted to protect from hurt, because they didn't treat me with the same sense of false graciousness.

Something dramatically damaging intercepted my emotions. I struggled to connect emotionally with traumatic situations, and I felt unable to process pain or explore my hurt and disappointment. I was eager to get over and through disappointment, and I refused to sit and stew in it, cry my eyes out for days, and position myself as a victim. Don't get me wrong, I would listen to your story about abuse, misfortune, and disappointment, but I lost the ability to feel empathy or compassion. I appeared robotic or immediately felt anger; there was nothing in the middle for me. It was a silent and invisible emotional transition, as though a shade had been pulled down at the window, darkening my room, my mind, and my emotions. I knew how to check out on others because I learned how to check out on myself, numb the pain, and move on.

Easy Prey

At the tender age of ten, he instructed me to lie down on the floor. He tugged at my pants, trying to pull them down. He coached me, saying, "tell me if it hurts, but don't be too loud." He fondled me but failed to physically penetrate me. I was sternly instructed, "DO NOT TELL!" I dreaded being alone with him. He was nice and nasty at the same time, he was a hero and a villain, and he made a victim of me. I clearly remember thinking to myself, *what was that thing…and why are you pushing it on me?*

My ten-year-old mind tried to process these conflicting messages, and my most burning questions were, *Does love physically hurt? Does love penetrate to your core, leaving you scared and conflicted? Does love hurt you in secret and smile at you publicly? Does love shame you, dare you to speak up when it hurts you, and never look back to apologize for the casualties it produced?*

Does love destroy you, never check your emotions, and never seek forgiveness or reconciliation? Perhaps love leaves you slowly decomposing, and you must find the tools, strength, and fortitude to push and fight through a violation that didn't come asking questions, but instead selfishly invaded your privacy, stole your innocence, and left you wondering how you could have been selected to bear such a cumbersome and cruel cross.

There is no fear in love. But perfect love drives out fear, because fear has to do with punishment. The one who fears is not made perfect in love.

—1 John 4: 18 (NIV)

There I was—a ten-year-old girl asking questions that no one could answer because they couldn't see what happened, couldn't grasp the horror I must have felt, or didn't know how to address the situation without exposing the truths that they were masking. Sometimes, in an effort to rescue someone else, you must first rescue yourself and address the shame you secretly hide. My brokenness escaped the notice of the adults around me because, they couldn't see me withering away. All the while, on the inside I was confused, conflicted, and silently learning how to ignore my pain and minimize what happened to me. We can't "fix" what we can't see—or maybe we refuse to fix what we can see because we are then forced to account for the brokenness within.

Scars are not limited to physical gashes and tears in the flesh that can be covered with cosmetics, masks, casts, Band-Aids, and gauze. Some scars take years to heal even when fresh air and time work in their favor. Some scars leave significant holes that can stunt your growth, paralyze your development, and stifle your ability to love, see clearly, and judge fairly. Some injuries leave you emotionally imprisoned because you don't have the capacity to heal or free yourself, and you feel too ashamed to seek help from others. All scars are not visible, and some can only be seen when you take your hand or your heart and reach inside another person to see their brokenness.

My own experience with brokenness taught me to minimize what happened to me because no one validated my pain, my experience, my story, or my disappointment. Then, as I matured, everyone else's concerns, fears, likes, and dislikes became more important than my own. My needs were secondary to the needs of those I cared for and wanted to please. I learned how to rationalize my feelings away while validating yours.

The offense committed against me permeated my mind and influenced all the decisions that I would later make regarding love and pain, acceptance and rejection, peace and conflict. But God used my experiences to show me and others that I had been broken to be blessed, and then given to the world to encourage others and remind them that they are not "damaged goods." This story is not designed to excite or entice, but to remind each person that, regardless of where you were lost due to trauma or violation, you can be found, rescued, wholly healed in the Lord, and returned to the right road.

And the God of all grace, who called you to his

eternal glory in Christ, after you have suffered a little while, will himself restore you and make you strong, firm, and steadfast.

—1 Peter 5: 10 (NIV)

Control

*Definition: The Power to Influence or Direct
Behavior or the Course of Events*

Gaining and regaining control are intentional actions,
but losing control can be subtle, and can go unnoticed.

When my godson, Punkin was a baby, I loved to hold
him close and rock him in my arms. I expected to hold
him all the time—I was probably spoiling him, but I
didn't want to admit it. When he was in my care or company, I felt obligated to rock him to sleep, soothe him
when he cried, and rescue him for others, and I didn't
want to see him upset. Sometimes his mother would say,
"Can you please put your Punkin to sleep?" I would
chuckle and respond, "Gladly!" I remember that one
time I walked several New York blocks holding him as I
tried to determine why he was crying. His mom drove
the car slowly alongside us, yelling out the window of

her car, "Is he still crying?" I was not a mother myself, and I did not have much experience with children, but my peers had children, so I picked up a few nuggets of wisdom from watching these parents over time. I prayed and walked for blocks, and then I got into the car to undress him. Perhaps he was too hot, and he couldn't tell us because he was only a few months old. When I pulled the shoe off his right foot, the cries slowly subsided. Poor fella—he'd flexed his toe and couldn't stretch it out once the shoe was tied on his foot. I felt like a good godmother that day—I had helped to solve the problem!

Before my daughter was born, I purchased a gliding rocking chair for her bedroom. I had convinced myself that I would sit down to rock her to sleep. In December of 2013, I began to rock her to sleep by accident—we rocked one emotionally stormy night, and it quickly turned into a nightly routine. Sometimes, I would go into my daughter's room and feel like a baby who needed to be rescued—those days, I would rock myself. She wasn't in my arms, she wasn't crying, and I wasn't feeding her, but I needed soothing. I would put her to sleep in her crib and sit in the rocking chair for hours, rocking and gliding back and forth. My face filled with tears that dripped from my chin, and as I dried them, I told myself, "You must get up from here and go turn the lights off downstairs and get ready for tomorrow." I just sat there in that one spot and rocked. Some nights I rocked myself to sleep, rocked until I felt better, and rocked until I couldn't rock anymore.

I put several miles on that chair, rocking and gliding and thinking. Recalling the hours, I spent gliding back and forth, forth and back over and over again, I see that perhaps the little girl within needed soothing, too.

He Hit Me

As a child, I was not good at mathematics. Mathematics was a thorn in my flesh from grade school through college and can still hurt me a bit today if I let it. I recall that at 13 years old, my report card would show below-average grades in mathematics. One night, after we received our report cards, my mother talked to me about my grades, and I dreaded the verbal scolding from my father. I remember that on that night I wore red stirrup pants and a red-and-white striped sweater as I sat in the family room watching television with my mother, hoping that night would be different while dreading the sound of my father's keys in the front door. Dad's home…

My parents discussed dinner, but before my dad ate his dinner, he wanted to discuss my report card. Let me reiterate that my parents sent me to Catholic school, which was costly, and that they did not accept failing grades, because they spent their hard-earned money so that I could get a good education and have an edge above the rest. My heart was pounding underneath my sweater as I heard my dad call, "Kim, come here!" I was petrified as I stood in the doorway. My father instructed me to sit down on the bed. Standing over me, he stated, "You got a 'D' in math. 'D' is for dumb and 'D' is for dog." I was trembling! He said, "You know that me and your Ma pay good money for you to go to that Catholic school and bring home good grades." He asked me, "What does 'D' stand for?" I hesitantly responded, "It also stands for door and Daddy, and I'm trying my hardest at math, it just isn't easy for me." Perhaps he didn't really want an answer to the question. He reached down to pick up the well-worn construction boot that he'd just taken off and raised the boot toward my head. I distinctly remember blocking the boot with my one hand and balling up my fist with the other. I must've landed one punch, but when he noticed that his nose was bleeding, he truly beat the stew out of me that night. Looking back at that night my dad was merely scaring me into getting better grades. He had no intentions on hitting me with the boot, but things appeared differently from my perspective.

After that rage-fueled beat-down because I was disrespectful to my father, I was confident that I would never rise up against my parents EVER again in any fashion. I was so physically hurt that I wasn't sure that I would see tomorrow. I remember sitting motionless in the corner thinking, what have I done? That night, my mother was upset with me because I hit my father. I'm sure he told her that I was a disgrace, and that she created this monster by spoiling me. That night, I was bitter and afraid because she didn't keep my father from hurting me. She didn't defend me, and she didn't diffuse the situation by saying, "Let's talk about this another time." That night, I was too frightened to fall asleep. I felt alone, and I was physically aching in pain. I went to my room and counted the coins in my small brown metal rectangular bank. I checked to see if I had enough money to take the

MTA #19 bus from the Bronx to Harlem, where I could live with my Godmother. After my father noticed that I was counting my coins, he threw three quarters at me and walked out of the room. He said, "You're looking for money to go, here you go…bye!"

I wanted to leave home, but I truly had nowhere to go. The safest place was at home with my family, but I felt uncomfortable there. I tried not to eat their food or use their water, but that couldn't last long, because I was still a child living in their home. When your safe place becomes a dreaded place, you know that you're in trouble. I felt like a stranger, the outsider in a room filled with my own things. My clothes were in the closet and dresser drawers, but I felt like I didn't belong there. I was becoming intimate with the feeling of rejection, and I learned how to cope and accommodate the feeling without knowing it.

My parents and siblings were upset with me for what seemed like months and were shocked that I had "defended" myself. My eldest brother said, "You do not hit your parents, and you had better apologize!" My younger brother asked, "What came over you? You don't do no crap like that—you're lucky Pop didn't kill you!" No one in my family took a moment to visit my scars, validate my pain, or acknowledge my disappointment and shock. It was simply my experience and my fault.

I can only recall receiving two beatings in my life, but this one was different. That night I drew a line in the sand, secretly declaring to myself that no man would put his hand on me and then tell me that he loved me. It was a contradiction and conflict that I couldn't rationalize— it hurt too much. There it was, resurfacing again, the same question for which my 10-year-old self-had sought the answer. How can love hurt you, and then not care enough to look back to express concern for the damage it caused? I asked the same question again as an adult when my husband packed a bag and left after we returned from our honeymoon.

Two of the same

Rewind 16 years earlier, when my first husband attempted to drag me by my long tresses. I went straight New York on him, and then called the police to come get him.

Fast Forward 27 years, when my second husband pushed me while I was pregnant with my daughter, I had no problem pushing him back. It was only a short flight of steps, and he wasn't hurt, but he was startled that I pushed him.

At 2AM on Palm Sunday morning, he decided that he would pay me back for attempted aggravated assault. I'd punched him in his face and smacked him with a laundry basket some 30 days earlier. I had been folding laundry, and my baby was splashing in the bathtub. I was coming out of a 7-day consecration period in which I had asked the Lord to pull back the covers and reveal all things to me that were hidden in the dark. Nine days earlier, he had asked for a divorce. That Sunday evening, he asked if I were going to give him a divorce. I answered, "Yes!" He rushed to find a steno pad to take notes and log the specifics of child support and visitation, and begged me not come after his business. He told me that he was leaving us again, but that this time, it was for good. He had set the date for his upcoming nuptials with a woman I knew—he hadn't wanted me to be upset when he introduced us. He also mentioned that he was moving to a gated community with her to live in their 3,000 square foot house. He went on to mention that I didn't do anything for him, and that he wouldn't miss me. That was the moment at which I emerged from my seated position, folding clothes, swinging the laundry basket. I was raged like a crazed woman—I had blacked out for a moment and couldn't calm myself down. I yelled,

"Get your things, and get the f@%k out of my house. How dare you speak to me like I owe you something and you're doing me a favor? I've been in the squeeze for years because of you. Get out!"

My heart raced and ached at the same time; my blood boiled; I was furious. I said every curse word I knew and created a few new ones. *How dare you keep doing this to me? How dare you continue to disrespect and discard me?* The hurt 10-year-old me was in the room. *How dare you keep me teetering on the edge? Here I am again…* When we married, I thought that my question had been answered, but I found myself back there again, searching for a definite and reasonable answer to a question that my 10-year-old self still asks. *How can love try to destroy you and still say it needs you?* Deep within myself, I knew that if he had put his hand on me in that moment, I would have sliced his gut to the white meat in retribution for every time I had felt defenseless and humiliated, and that then I would call the police and emergency medical services. My daughter saved both of us that night.

These themes keep repeating themselves…

I've shared many details about my life, but not much about my marriages. After the first divorce, I was single for 12 years, happily loving my freedom and growth as a woman. Then, I decided to make a calculated change to marry my love, and all the while my love silently calculated the benefits of marrying me. My first husband personified how I thought love should appear-- caring, affirming, and affectionate, while the behavior of the second forced me to revisit the same feelings of loneliness after He Hit me. He turned on me, turned against me, bullied me, and uncovered me to protect himself when his anger manifested. He refused to address the darkness lurking within the walls of his mind and heart. I'll admit that I wanted to feel protected, wanted, loved, and appreciated for my efforts, but there was no value there. Yes, I did get a "thank you" for cooking dinner, and cards on Mother's Day, wedding anniversaries, birthdays, and Christmas, but what was I getting when there was no holiday? We shared a few laughs, but there was always a lingering disrespect in his condescending and inappropriate comments. I constantly lived with a sense of anxiety that I might say or do something to crank up the monster within him… it didn't take much.

Relationship Principle: Some people never witness a healthy and loving relationship. Therefore, in the absence of a healthy modeled relationship, they may explore many unknowns all "in the pursuit of love". Retrospectively, I physically exchanged licks with both my ex-husbands. What did I see that caused me to feel the need to fight?

Broken, Blessed, and Given

This August is about coming out of the blind spots—breaking curses and bad behaviors that were passed down through generations. The blind spot negatively impacts visibility and, it can also be the very thing we hide behind and use as a crutch when we're not ready to face the truth about who we are. Failing to openly communicate the hard truths that constantly plagued my mind was heavy in my soul.   For many generations, my family ignored the hurt and violation committed against their bodies, suppressed the injustices raging in their minds, and told themselves stories to cope with the dysfunction. We constantly live with a trail of brokenness passed down through generations, layered with hurt and deception, and covered with "love and hugs," while the root of the issue is always overlooked. We often face what's hanging off the tree, but fail to address what's buried at the root, fueling the fruit. I was in conflict with myself—

I constantly encouraged other women to live out their fullest potential while failing to address the brokenness preventing me from truly living my own. Writing this memoir explores the culmination of my fears, while highlighting my courage and demonstrating the faith that pushed me to be who God created me to be.

The Functioning Handicap

Some time later, Jesus went up to Jerusalem for one of the Jewish festivals. [2]Now there is in Jerusalem near the Sheep Gate a pool, which in Aramaic is called Bethesda[a] and which is surrounded by five covered colonnades. [3]Here a great number of disabled people used to lie—[4] the blind, the lame, the paralyzed. [5]One who was there had been an invalid for thirty-eight years. [6] When Jesus saw him lying there and learned that he had been in this condition for a long time, he asked him, "Do you want to get well?"[7] "Sir," the invalid replied, "I have no one to help me into the pool when the water is stirred. While I am trying to get in, someone else goes down ahead of me."[8] Then Jesus said to him, "Get up! Pick up your mat and walk."[9]At once the man was cured; he picked up his mat and walked. —John 5: 5–9 (NIV)

Just like the man at the pool of Bethesda in the Bible, we wait for help, but make excuses when help arrives. We accommodate the dysfunctions resulting from our dis-EASE. The man at Bethesda lay at the pool for thirty-eight years with his dis-EASE. He lay there for such a long time that he learned to make excuses for why he was still unchanged while accommodating the debilitating results of the disease. Jesus asked him, "Do you want to be made well?" The sick man answered Him with the excuse that "he had no man to put him in the pool when the water is stirred." Aren't we like this unnamed man at the pool—quick to identify that we are stagnant, yet we blame our lack of response to our illness on someone else? Isn't it like us to find an excuse or defend our sickness instead of answering the question, "Do you want to be made well?" We have a false sense of security that forces us deeper into the dis-EASE when we blame others for our present condition. Being unaccountable supports a victimized mentality and validates our deformed mental posture, and thus we make excuses for the sickness and the stench that the dis-EASE leaves behind instead of promoting our own healing and moving forward!

The residue left from my molestation was shame and guilt. I constantly shamed myself because of what had happened to me, rather than acknowledging that it wasn't my fault. I had to be careful not to make accommodations for the residue, telling myself that I wasn't lovable, devaluing myself with harsh criticism, putting the emotional needs of others before my own, and sometimes pushing others away because I didn't want them to see my inner wounds and scars. Dis-EASE can disconnect you from your own experiences, forcing you to become numb and to detach from situations that should emotionally engage you.

DIARY ENTRY

Friday, January 23rd, 2015 —10:21 PM

Happy New Year—for real! I haven't journaled in over three years. I married in April 2012, and had a baby in August 2013. She turned 17 months three days ago, and I love her so much! It's the beginning of a new year, and I'm living as a single woman. My husband moved out on Wednesday, December 24, 2014—Christmas Eve— and my mother-in-law passed away two days later on Friday, December 26th. That was an extremely strange and hard time to see clearly, and sometimes it seems as though the conflict was never fully resolved. I'm in a tough situation, and one that I had never hoped to live— raising a child by myself, footing the bills, and carrying the weights of life alone. Sometimes I miss my husband, but I so appreciate the peace.

My life has taken an unexpected turn. In March 2014,

the Spirit of the Lord spoke to me while I walked the aisles of the local grocery store and said, "By the end of the year, you'll know what you need to do." The end of the year was 24 days ago.

What a year that was!

DIARY ENTRY

Weakness —7ᵗʰ Street, October 2017

Today I feel weak. I feel weak and weary from trying to figure out if God has left me alone here to find a way to survive. I feel weak from continuously reviewing the details, trying to discover new ways to answer to the old question—*How did I get here?*

I'm heartbroken and filled with questions about the "how's" of my life. How did I arrive at this impasse? I don't mean a mode of transportation or a geographical location. I'm talking about this emotional and uncertain state of trying to constantly examine where I went wrong, and rethinking what I could have done to avoid this destination. This is the place that I have desperately avoided my entire life, yet at which I still arrived. Perhaps this stop needed to be a part of my journey to the final destination. My decisions were intentional after lots of prayer, reviewing facts, and self-evaluation. While I am a spontaneous shopper, I did not exercise that same spontaneity and carelessness in my life decisions. I operated with thorough planning and safe, cautious, clever, and calculated thoughts filled with truth and honesty. Yet I'm still here. *How did I get here?*

In this vulnerable and naked state, I felt weak and frustrated. I wanted to turn off the phone, the lights, the television, my brain, my reality, and the truth. I wanted to turn off the world I lived in. I wasn't depressed, but the constant self-scrutiny weakened and exhausted me more each day, because I needed to know how I had arrived here. *I need an answer!* I wanted to drive out into the wilderness and scream at the top of my lungs, hoping that someone would hear me and rescue me from this pain, this void, these tears, this hurt, and this disappointment. But the truth is that I was already screaming in a wilderness, and although people were around, no one could hear my cries or help me. It was then that the

Word of the Lord came to me and encouraged me that God's strength is made perfect is my weakness.

But he said to me, "My grace is sufficient for you, for my power is made perfect in weakness." Therefore, I will boast all the more gladly about my weaknesses, so that Christ's power may rest on me.

—2 Corinthians 12: 9 (NIV)

THIS August

This August, I asked myself many questions. I felt determined to obtain a deeper level of comprehension and to truly embrace how I really got here, even if the answers were embarrassing, frightening, humiliating, or even incriminating. I'm always asking questions, reviewing the answers, and sometimes scrutinizing the outcomes, but I'm always determined to live with my final decision and to make lemon treats from all the lemons life may serve me. My therapist asked hard questions, but I was prepared to give honest answers.

Question: Why did you stay so long?

Answer: I don't think I stayed too long. I stayed because I have a family, because I loved this man, and because I'm not a fan of giving up or quitting without trying or fighting. I'm not a coward! I stayed because love waits…

I took ownership of my failure and disconnect. I constantly told myself things that I could have done or said differently, and as long as I could emotionally face the dysfunctional craziness, I stayed. Over these years, I had only blacked out once in an unforgettable rage. My goodness, it wasn't a good look for me, and when I came to myself and my blood began to simmer, I thought to myself, "I'm in the wrong relationship with the wrong person." I was extremely frustrated, and I wanted him to understand that I deeply loved him and that I wanted the best for our family. That was the answer that I gave to the therapist that day, but in truth, I stayed because I wanted my daughter to have a chance at growing up in a loving home with two parents. I stayed because I wanted to believe that all we had endured until that point was worth it, and that this relationship could stand the test of time. I stayed because it's what you do when you're married, and when you believe that God has joined you together. I stayed because I was trying to outlive the prophetic words that had indicated that this marriage had come to an end 17 months earlier. I wanted to defy the writing on the wall. I stayed because something in my broken self desperately wanted to believe that he loved me, that he wanted his family, and that through our total surrender to God, he would heal us and we could work it out.

I knew that I was being robbed of love and respect, but I couldn't find the logical and rational answers to explain it. I beat myself up and told myself, *It's your New York attitude keeping you from getting the best parts of him. You're too dang astute; you ask too many questions, and should have worked on being dumber and less aware than you are.* In essence, I was telling myself to dim my light so that his could shine. Dimming my light wasn't an option, because my light shone even when I didn't try to make it shine. I desperately tried to dot every "i" and cross every "t," but nothing seemed to satisfy him. Arguments brewed over money, cars, food, laundry, how and when to pay bills, family members, the television, the ceiling fan, sex, intimacy, the air conditioner, the heat… EVERYTHING! It was a rough few years, and nothing ever seemed to wholly sustain us. There was no peace and no agreement, and God consistently spoke to me, warning me of what was lurking in the dark. While conflicting thoughts about the successes and failures of my marriage constantly flooded my mind, I knew that this season would be lonely and daunting, because I had to face the truth. This August forced me to dive into the bowels of myself and to acknowledge the unresolved and unexamined things that happened in my past which were hindering my future. This book is not about a strong, successful, and beautiful woman who was victimized, but rather it's about a beautifully vibrant woman learning to acknowledge and appreciate her value and learning her boundaries and enforcing them with others while sustaining her voice and emotionally connecting with equals who would never stifle her voice or muffle her God-given life.

Principle: There is safety in truth.

Devastation

I have never claimed to be smart, perfect or a great person, but I have ascertained that I am fair. While the term "fair" is relative, it holds a tremendous amount of weight in my self-evaluation. Being fair often means that I have given others the benefit of the doubt in situations that didn't merit this kind-hearted and hopeful attempt to see what wasn't there. I know what you're thinking—who am I to say that someone or something doesn't merit favor or Grace? But sometimes you must digest things as they appear, and you don't subject the facts to your filtering process. One of the downsides to always giving the benefit of the doubt is that you may ignore what's blatantly obvious, and you may replace the truth with your own rationale, which can ultimately transform your personal boundaries.

Giving the benefit of the doubt has sometimes caused

me to reject the truth as I optimistically attempted to find the good in situations where it did not exist, and where the good wasn't actively being pursued. There were many instances in which I gave the benefit of the doubt and told myself that I had "found" the "good" while ignoring the facts, and I simply hoped that the facts were a figment of my creative imagination. It seems likely that denial or willful blindness was hidden in my "benefit of the doubt" processing.

In the dating stages of relationship, you tend to share stories about your past relationships, expectations, future hopes, and aspirations. I was open, and honestly shared these things. It seemed ironic and confusing at the same time, but I was talking to my friend, so it was a no-holds-barred chat. Once united in matrimony, the facts were flipped and used as weapons against me. There were those conversations that started as intimate chats between newlyweds, and turned into an assault against my character, as though my love was trying to shame me and tear me down with insults. I remember one evening when we were sitting in the home office, and he asked, "Do you think he really liked you?" I confusedly replied, "Who are you talking about?" He responded, "Dorsey Fitzgerald," and I recall asking, "Why are you bringing him up, and how is he relevant to this conversation or relationship?" His response was, "He's relevant because I want to talk about it!" I was thoroughly taken aback by the level of abrupt rudeness in that conversation, and I sat silently for a few seconds trying to figure out where the conversation was going. I got up from the desk chair and walked into the bedroom. He followed, asking, "Do you think Dorsey Fitzgerald played you? Do you think he really loved you?" He followed these questions with a little chuckle, and then he said, "Dorsey Fitzgerald may have wanted to hit it, but he didn't want to go home with you and pay the bills." He went on to ask, "Do you think he played you?" For two seconds, I thought to myself, *young man, you are playing yourself with this immature line of questioning.* I responded, "We are married now—why do you care what his intentions were? That was a part of my past. This is our present and future, and WE should be focused on US and not Dorsey Fitzgerald. I'm sure he's not thinking about you. I shared that with you long ago, but suddenly you're divisively using information that I voluntarily shared against me." The conversation was not filled with the love of a nurturing husband protecting his wife from incident or accident. Instead, I was thrown to the emotional wolves, and my value was cheapened with each sentence that followed. Perhaps that was how he was feeling—having regrets about his new marriage.

Anyone who knows me is familiar with the swiftness of my comebacks, and likely just said, "I know that Kim got at him." But I was too stunned, and I took this one for the team, because I knew that my response would have cut him to his core. This was the first conversation that both troubled and puzzled me, and caused me to ask myself, *What kind of loving husband speaks to his wife in such a derogatory and inflammatory way?*

Although we were on speaking terms, and although I was engaged in our conversation, I was mentally absent, silent, and perplexed for many days after that conversation. I was hurt by his words, and I felt humiliated as I tried to accept that I wasn't living with someone who liked me, and who could not therefore like himself. *If he could speak to me with such venomous words, perhaps this is how he thought of me. Perhaps he thought I was a trick he was going to turn, getting what he wanted and moving on.* Did this conversation reveal who he was—his intentions for "finding" me? Did he feel unlucky, or was he having second thoughts about his decision to marry me? A plethora of questions flooded my mind. I was shocked, insulted, and downright angered that I had been handled so carelessly. It took many weeks for me to process the exchange, to forgive my husband, and to put the incident behind me. I'm not one of those people who believe that things just happen—I believe there is significance in most things that happen, but that we don't always catch the significance immediately. In that moment, I believed that God was using these harsh conversations to get my attention so that I could see my true attachments, and could see the demonic spirits and attacks I was up against. He simply responded by telling me that I had taken his words too personally and that he wasn't going to sugar-coat the truth for me. I felt unearthed, uprooted, and dismantled, all the while reciting to myself as I became more insecure, *this is not how friends communicate. What "truth" was he truly trying to convey?*

Mentally depleted from constantly replaying this message and trying to discern the truth, I decided that he could be intimidated by me. *Otherwise,* I reasoned, *I'm not sure why he'd intentionally try to hurt me.* I was confident that the enemy was trying to break me down.

In June 2012, I was falsely accused of being in an adulterous relationship with someone who I had never met for dinner. Naturally, there was no proof to confirm the nonexistent affair. On the Friday night in question, I had gone to the hair salon, Burlington Coat Factory, and a tiny eatery with a girlfriend. Luckily, I had retained receipts, and confirmed that my girlfriend would vouch for me to prove my whereabouts. *Lies!* Later, the accusations turned to me being in contact with a man with whom I had previously had a long-distance relationship. I was taunted to give up his phone number. The mental battery continued throughout the night, and I was forced to discuss a dinner date that had not taken place. I was threatened with divorce, labeled a liar, and accused of protecting an individual with whom I hadn't spoken in years. The truth is that my husband was entertaining a woman from *his* past, and together they determined to make me guilty only to exonerate themselves from their harsh reality. Sometimes, the party seems justifiable if someone will party with you, but if you party alone, it's no fun. This is called "projecting."

Projecting is commonly undertaken by a guilty party who needs to defend himself against his own unconscious impulses or qualities by denying the existence of these qualities in himself and attributing them to others. I'm not sure if this should be deemed "double-minded" or "flat-out lying," but it laid the foundation for what was to come.

A double minded man is unstable in all his ways.

—James 1:8 (KJV)

It was 12:29 AM on Saturday, December 29, 2012. I was preparing for bed after we had arrived home from the movies, and I reminisced about the two hotdogs that I had enjoyed at the movie. Everyone who knows me knows that I do not eat hotdogs, but for some reason, the sight of that hotdog had provoked an unexplainable craving. The week before, a colleague had hinted that I could be pregnant, but I told her that the well was drying up. We laughed, and she recommended that I take a test, suggesting that it might pose the answer to my sudden fatigue, missed period, and random cravings. That night, I dared to take the test that I had reluctantly purchased, and I hid in the closet, asking myself if I was prepared for the answer. I recall taking the test, placing the instrument on the bathroom countertop, and then waiting with bated breath to see the (-/+) sign appear. I looked at the test, and then I looked away. I wrapped my hair and tried desperately not to look at the test again. I organized my jewelry in the armoire to buy time, and then walked back over to the countertop. Those few moments seemed like a lifetime. When I looked back at the test, I could see the results, but I read the box to make sure that I fully understood what the plus sign meant. My heart sank—I'm pregnant. I wasn't sure how to respond. I had mixed emotions. I took a few minutes to collect myself, exited the bathroom, and brought the pregnancy test to my husband. He instructed me to turn on the light, and then he asked, "Does this mean that you're pregnant?" I responded quickly, "Yes, but I'll take a second test tomorrow, because this thing could be wrong." Immediately he insulted me by insinuating that the baby had been fathered by another man, and that he was not the father. The wind was knocked out of me— what a blow to suffer! *Who says that to his wife?* All the excitement I should have felt at the onset of this pregnancy was stolen from me by my husband's immaturity. I got in the bed, rolled over, and cried myself to sleep. I felt robbed and violated—*This thief stole my happy moment!* You're probably thinking, *Oh, she overreacted*, but when most of your "good" moments are shrouded with negativity from an insensitive wise guy, you start shrinking inside, and decide to keep things to yourself. What's the value of sharing the good stuff with someone who can only see things from a negative and limited viewpoint?

I made plans to visit the doctor to confirm the pregnancy, and to see how far along I was. On January 2nd, I went to the doctor to give a urine sample, and as I exited the restroom, the doctor, nurse, and nurse's assistants were clapping. I smiled, but I was still confused by the news. It was indeed good news that we we're having a baby and the well hadn't dried up, but I now had to share my shoe money with my baby, LOL! I went into the examination room and began to perspire profusely. The doctor asked, "Are you okay? You look pale." Before I could answer, the doctor rushed out of the examination room to bring me a bottle of water. I wanted to cry and celebrate simultaneously. The emotional conflict was growing inside of me, but at that moment, I didn't have the words to construct my thoughts. Actually, I was excited by my pregnancy, because silently I had given up on childbearing. So many foul and unscrupulous events had transpired that I was unsure that I wanted to have a baby with my husband.

23 days after learning of my pregnancy—still amazed by the fact that my baby was the size of a lentil bean, an over-blown conversation fueled with anger and hurt about opening a window in the guest bedroom resulted in my husband pushing me through a doorway. I stumbled backward over a table in the hallway as my husband told me that I was "in the way and needed to be moved." I cried for many days after this incident, asking myself, *Where did I go wrong?* and *What could I have said differently?* I wondered if I wanted to bring a baby into this dysfunctional environment. The one thing that held my confidence was that I didn't warrant violent hands being placed on me. While I processed my feelings and replayed the event over in my head, I refused to embrace the truth. The truth was that he put his hands on a pregnant woman. I dialed 911, and then blamed myself for the path that the conversation had taken. I vowed that it was my fault, and that I would do all that I could to keep "us" from physical altercation in the future.

Dr. Kay, the obstetrician was thoughtful, and equally committed to this emotional journey with me because we had 7 years invested in this doctor/patient relationship. We knew I'd have a scheduled c-section, but she had concerns about the amount of tension at home because you could cut through it with a knife when my entire family showed up at the doctor visit.

My pregnancy was phenomenal! No morning sickness, no dizziness, no uncomfortable or sleepless nights, no headaches, no pains… only tingling fingers and toes the entire third trimester. The tingles drove me crazy, because I couldn't type at work without my fingers going numb, and I couldn't rest my feet too long in one position without feeling pins and needles. The doctors told me that I was a high-risk pregnancy because of my age, but they were impressed with our negative screenings for down syndrome, cystic fibrosis, sickle cell disease, and spina bifida. We're thankful that our baby girl arrived without complications and has thrived since birth.

During the last two months of my pregnancy, I was disappointed by the lack of concern that my husband gave me. I felt baffled and confused that he would leave home to care for loved ones overnight while his pregnant wife stayed home alone with the dog. I was puzzled by how he could go watch a sporting game for hours, and never send a text to check on us or send a text 5 minutes before he headed home. I was befuddled by the response "you got this" when I expressed feelings of hurt and disappointment. *Are you just going to leave me like this? Do you realize that I'm weeks… days away from having a baby? Do you really care about me? How does your conscience allow you to leave me alone for days at a time, telling me that I don't need you?* The truth is that I felt unloved, unappreciated, devalued, rejected, and lost in this relationship. I didn't know my place in the relationship anymore. One morning during my drive into the office, I shamefully admitted to a good friend that my husband was having an affair. The tears filled my eyes, and the phone line was silent. She replied, "Oh Kim!" I promised her that I wouldn't say a thing, but God had shown me something in a dream, and He never lied to me. It was only a matter of time before the truth emerged. I started giving him the benefit of the doubt, making excuses, telling myself that I was hormonal, and that he was nervous about the new baby, because life was about to change tremendously for us. While all of these things were true, it was also true that he was pre-occupied with a new relationship, and he was splitting his time between work, home, and their rendezvous.

On Tuesday, August 20, 2013, we arrived at the hospital at 5:30 AM to meet our baby girl. It was dark outside, but I was excited to see the hospital, knowing that I was about to meet the baby who we would call Kayla. Security personnel smiled with us as we entered the building, the valet took the car, and I remembered passing a family in the doorway as we entered into the hospital. The woman mentioned the size of my stomach— "Wow, that's a big one!" I was having a 9-pound baby, and I was nervous about how they were going to get my sweet girl out of my body. The thought of big needles inserted into my back and intravenous lines inserted into my wrist worried me terribly. The anesthesiologist, the nurses, and the doctors crowded into my room to ask questions, and then mentioned that they might not be able to deliver the baby today, because my lungs didn't sound good. I looked over at Dr. Kay with confusion, worried because the anesthesiologist seemed to be calling the shots. I went from calling the anesthesiologist "Doctor" to calling him by his first name, and I asked everyone to step out of the room except my obstetrician. The tears welled up in my eyes as I asked her, "how could this be happening to me?" I want to meet my baby today, not Thursday. She explained that they feared losing me on the operating table because my lungs were not operating at full capacity, and they weren't confident my breathing would sustain me through the surgery.

I looked at the IV in my wrist and said, "I need to have my baby today, I don't have enough guts to return on Thursday to have this reinserted into my wrist." They gave me a cup of ice and told me to eat up while they came up with a game-plan to medicate me in order for me to safely have the baby. The pulmonologist knocked on the door and entered the room. He introduced himself, pulled out his stethoscope, and listened to my lungs, telling me, "You don't sound good." I began to cry because I didn't want to die, and I didn't want to wait until Thursday to meet my baby. I was upset with my doctor, because she listened to my lungs weekly, and never mentioned that they sounded weak. I was also mad at her because she couldn't deliver my baby, and had to return to her practice to attend to other patients. I asked her, "Dr. Kay, are you going to leave me like this?" Her countenance fell, and she answered, "Yes, but I'll come and see you tomorrow." I could have screamed. My husband pulled up a chair at the foot of the hospital bed and asked, "So, what are you going to do? I'm sorry—what can I do but wait? I don't have a choice in the matter, as all the decisions have been made for me." I looked down at the IV in my wrist, and I heard him say, "You're never there for me!" I was thinking to myself, *This dude would ruin a wet dream—just let me have a moment without making everything about you.* I looked up at him and stupidly asked, "What are you talking about?" I already knew the answer. He said, "I'm always there for you, but you're never there for me." I looked over at him and asked, "Are you talking about me buying you a car? Now is not the time for this discussion." He responded, "We will have the discussion when I want to have it." I sternly replied, "Not today—my freaking life is on the line, the doctors are not sure if I'm going to live to meet the baby who has stretched me in all directions, and you're worried about a car I won't buy?" *Bye, boy!* If I hadn't known before, I knew in that moment that this man was not on my side. How selfish could one person be? I smiled for my parents who had traveled over 800 miles from New York to be with us, and tried to remain joyful because I knew that my spiritual mother was in transit to this hospital from New York to meet the baby. I needed to have this baby today. I also felt the need to put forward a smiling façade for the doctors, because I didn't want them to sense my hostile marital situation and take my baby from me. The nurse crept into my room while I was alone and asked, "What's wrong with him?" I responded, "Nothing, he's merely an asshole." She followed up by asking if I was okay. I was petrified, and I thought to myself, they must have caught on to the craziness.

Then, at 3:29 PM, I met my sweetest 6 lbs, and 13 ounce blessing.

I'm not sure when or how you access devastation. Is it before the storm hits, or after you analyze the injury, loss, and ruin caused by the storm? Perhaps it's after the tears, regret, and disappointment caused by not knowing what caused the breakdown in the relationship. Accommodating devastation can be a daily or lifetime rehearsal if you skillfully teach yourself to hold it together outwardly while you collapse internally. How can you effectively evaluate truth when you consistently fail to expose the lie?

I was devastated. I wasn't devastated by one thing in particular, but rather, I was saddened by my husband's lack of true love and concern, the insults, the disregard, and the disrespect. I was devastated by the overwhelming reality in which I lived. *This is horrifying!* Here I was again, asking the same question my 10-year-old self-had asked—*How does love perform so recklessly and never look back to see the destruction it caused?* I soon realized that even if the destruction had been spelled out on tablets of clay, it would have been easy to read but difficult to comprehend without a transformed mind.

Missed Education – Communication

You should have told me that I wasn't strong enough. You should have communicated to me that there would be moments of manipulation and deception. Why didn't you wake me up to the fact that prayer and fasting alone are not enough to invoke change? Is there a recipe for a successful marriage? Are godliness, maturity, and discipline the "right" ingredients? What else is needed—honesty, maybe? At what temperature do you prepare this thing—do you fix it on warm, or let it simmer for years on cold? What are the proper measurements of grace, mercy, and balance to bring this relationship to a steady boil? Tell me… what's the secret to a healthy marriage?

As for God, his way is perfect: The Lord's word is flawless; He shields all who take refuge in Him.

— Psalm 18:30 (NIV)

What I know with confidence is that God will speak to you in ways that humans cannot. I do not believe He leaves His children in limbo or in the wilderness without direction or answers for months or years. I do, however, believe that a consecrated life is necessary to clearly hear and understand God's voice and direction. Now, while my previous statement may sound like "church" rhetoric, I should add that while meditating on the scriptures is right and necessary, it is not enough. I believe we can read the Bible, faithfully attend and serve in our local church, and suffer naturally while claiming victory. In order to have a whole and healthy life, you must address skeletal concealments, past decisions, generational curses, and familial habits. It is crucial that we take a deep dive into the drivers of our behavior to fully understand what impacts our decisions.

I recall having frightening dreams as a young girl. I engaged in battle, fighting for my life against life-sized concealed enemies that I couldn't defeat. Instead, the more I tried to destroy them, the bigger they grew. As a young girl, I recall knowing the moment at which my paternal grandmother passed away—I could sense something was "missing." As an adult, I once looked at my maternal grandmother and knew that she would only live five days before passing away.   There were months and seasons when growing as a babe in Christ in which I didn't want to sleep at night—I was frightened by the level of demonic activity exposed in my dreams, and it was both alarming and confusing. As I matured in Christ, the Lord began to communicate with me about imps, strongholds, and identifying which demons were in operation. He started communicating with me via the water bug. I saw the water bug in my dreams and in person. In person, you immediately think these bugs are a sign of filth or dirt, and perhaps a deep clean of the house is in order.   When I see these bugs inside or outside, I think the same, but as I matured in God, I learned He was using something that paralyzed me in the natural world to convey a spiritual message.

But God hath chosen the foolish things of the

world to confound the wise; and God hath chosen
the weak things of the world to confound the
things which are mighty. -1 Corinthians 1:27 (KJV)

I do not like to kill insects by smashing or squashing them. I don't want direct contact with any bug, and especially not a water bug. I'd prefer to spray them from a distance and pray they take a drink of the poison, and I'll cover them up or call for someone to rescue me from the monster. In short, none of these methods guarantee the death of the insect, instead they only slow its death. What I know today is that God loves and is concerned about us, and that He communicates with us in ways that we can personally understand. God is communicating with you, shielding you, encouraging you, and leading you so that even when friends and family may not always comprehend or agree with God's methods of communicating with you, you are confident in the direction of God's voice.

While on my honeymoon, walking back to the hotel, my eyes met with a water bug on the sidewalk near a lamppost. I screamed, "Did you see that?" Then I went cold – frozen, stuck with one foot on the sidewalk and the other in the street. My heart started beating quickly, and I could feel the thumping vibration through my shirt. I told myself, *Calm down*. He tugged at my hand and pulled me onward as I briefly held up foot traffic. I started sweating, and I repeated, "Did you see that?" He calmly stated, "It's just a bug—it doesn't mean anything!" Later, he asked, "Do you think that the bug has some meaning for us?" I simply replied, "Yes!" But I knew the water bug was code for me… not for him.

God doesn't lie. I was startled by the water bug on Thursday the 19th, and the flight home on Saturday the 21st was very disturbing. My husband listed my insecurities and told me I wasn't going to be a good wife but assured me that he was instructed to stay the course regardless of what he had learned about me. He told me we would learn some things about each other, and that I wouldn't support him, but he should stay the course. This random rant continued all the way from the gate in

Las Vegas to the baggage claim in Charlotte, through lunch, and then culminated in a question when we arrived at home. "What do you think about that?" I thought I was being tricked or bamboozled! I wasn't sure how to answer that question without being offensive, and I felt confused and scared. I felt as though someone else may have better known how to answer the question, because I was clueless. I went out on a limb and answered, "I'm not really sure what I'm responding to, because it sounded like rambling to me." Well, that comment sparked the first argument. We had only been home from the honeymoon two hours when he packed a small bag and went to stay with his mother because, as he said, I wasn't ready for marriage. After he left, he called back to say, "You know I love you, right?"

I was flabbergasted. In that moment, the initial thought of annulling this 168-old hour marriage was birthed. Above all, I realized the sighting of the water bug two days earlier had been a warning of impending battle.

Camouflage

Camouflage is the use of any combination of materials, coloration, or illumination for concealment, either by making animals or objects hard to see, or by disguising them as something else.

I credit my mother with saying, "What don't come out in the wash, will come out in the rinse." While my mother says that she never said that phrase, I find truth in the statement, and credit her for introducing me to this age-old wisdom. In essence, the statement implies that the truth will come out eventually—it may take some time, but it will eventually be unmasked. Earlier in this narrative, I addressed my experience with the water bug. Over the years, the water bug has brought me warnings of impending fights, demonic activity, plots and strategies against me, and indications of all-out war. God has also allowed me to see these bugs dead with legs up, peeled apart and totally obliterated, standing still, and running away in fright. My first real understanding of warfare began when I began to comprehend how God communicated with me. I dare not say that God dealt with me in an unconventional way, because He addresses each of His children uniquely, and we have the responsibility to sit still and cultivate what He shares with us. Just as we maintain our relationships with earthly people, we must maintain our relationship with our Creator.

In March 2014, I dreamt of an office plant on a colleague's desk, and out of that plant marched five water bugs. These water bugs were visually different in size and texture. Their skin was the same color and texture as the office plant, but they were slightly healthier and faster than a "normal" water bug.

Here I was in the middle of the night dreaming about water bugs climbing out of a plant in broad daylight in the office that no one could see except me. I was confused in my dream, and even more confused when I woke up and tried to fully understand why God was showing me that the enemy was hiding in plain sight. One month later, there was a restack at the office. A restack is a fancy way to describe a seat change. I recall my seat being changed on a Friday, and I was excited about the new seat until I noticed the office plant from my dream had been repositioned and now sat directly to my left—just as it was in my dream. In my shock, I called over a colleague to confirm the plant had been relocated over the weekend. He confirmed that it had been relocated, and I sat at my desk with tears in my eyes, shaking my head and saying to the Lord, "Here we go again." I sat next to the plant from April 2014 until May 2016.

23 months God sat me next to a plant which signified

that the truths and secrets purposely hidden from me would intentionally be revealed. The plant was a constant reminder that war was raging, but that God had given me the results of the operational plan, if I would be patient and wait on Him. When my seat was moved again in May 2016, the plant was moved as well, but this time it was no longer in front of me—instead it was behind me. This may read like a story of coincidence and accident, but I know God strategically set me up to clearly see what He was divinely doing in my life.

For there is nothing hidden that will not be disclosed, and nothing concealed that will not be known or brought out into the open.

— Luke 8:17 (NIV)

As a baby in the Lord, God warned me in the same way, but He didn't use water bugs—instead, He used other forms to which I could relate, and which woke me up to the truth. The moral of this story is that God will keep you out of harm's way and will reveal the surprises that are lurking in the dark. God is a protector and a keeper of the mind. I spent weeks seeking God for direct answers, and spent long nights trying to comprehend the events of my life. God spoke to me and let me know He was shielding me from humiliation, and that He put a hedge of protection around me and had lifted a standard against the enemy. The weapons may be formed, but they won't prosper.

Question: How can you be on the same team with someone, trust them, and watch them consistently betray you?

The Thing

This thing has truly turned my world upside down, and I'm convinced that broken people can only thrive together until one person actively seeks to be fixed, to be better, and to be whole. This thing is both deceptive and divisive—it has sought to destroy me from the beginning, and has never truly loved me or treated me as an individual. I'm reminded of a popular 80's movie titled "The Thing" in which the primary antagonist, a parasitic extraterrestrial lifeform, assimilates other organisms and in turn imitates them. Isn't it just like the enemy to infiltrate and move onto the minds of God's people to cause them to miss out on a better life?

For the weapons of our warfare are not carnal, but mighty through God to the pulling down of strong holds; 5 Casting down imaginations, and every high thing that exalteth itself against the knowledge of

God, and bringing into captivity every thought to the obedience of Christ. -2 Corinthians 10: 4-5 (KJV)

A stronghold is an area of darkness within our mind or personality that causes ongoing spiritual, emotional, and behavioral problems. A stronghold is a lie that we have allowed to distort or confuse our thinking, and such a lie can gain a foothold in our mind and then in our behavior. If we allow a lie to reside within, that lie, like a seed, will produce its fruit, which will distort the way we see and think. Truth overcomes every lie! As Christians, the spiritual armor we first put on is Truth. Only then are we instructed to put on the full Armor of God, that we might stand against the devices and strategies of the Devil—we begin with Truth. I believe that, as women, we must put on the Truth of God's Word, and we must then deal with the truth of every experience that brought us to this moment. Each one of us has had an experience that has proven to be a stronghold in our lives, but such hardship can push you into healthy living if you let it go. **The thing** doesn't have you—instead, you're clutching onto it! You're trying to live a whole life, yet the baggage you're dragging with you toward each milestone, each experience, each relationship, and each job is keeping you broken and cracked... let **the thing** go!

Being in Control vs. Being in Charge

Being in charge is about surrendering your control to something larger than you. Being in control is about managing and manipulating every detail to fix an outcome in your favor. Once, as I faced ligation and was toiling with the shame associated with the case, I began to recognize the hesitation that "the thing" birthed in me while I anticipated the outcome of "the thing". The litigation worked out in my favor, as God showed me that it would, but I had come face-to-face with the palpable and undeniable truth that I was growing beyond a place that held me hostage for years and was growing past the fear that "the thing" would continue to control me. I was blossoming, turning into a beautiful flower by giving up my own control in order to be in charge—truly, this vulnerable and unwavering position was the driver of my growth and transition.

Understanding and embracing that "the thing" wasn't bigger than me and didn't have control over me—the knowledge hit me like a car coming to a screeching halt at a red light after moving at 60 miles per hour. I recognized I owned the tools to unlock my freedom; I possessed the ability to stop grieving over what I thought I had lost in the divorces, in the molestation, in the abuse, in the disappointments; and I decided to strengthen what God had allowed to remain. God doesn't make mistakes. The light had finally come on—I would only be as great as the thing that I'd given power to incarcerate me. I was fighting to get past the past, but I continually emotionally relived the stories that kept me victimized. I internally regurgitated the events that happened to me, and this regurgitation forced me to view things with limited sight.

Being in charge challenged me to forgive the hurt people who had hurt me. Being in charge caused me to trace the roots of my own brokenness, which I'd toted around like a Louis Vuitton bag, and to face them head-on. I needed to count the cost of my own poor decisions and mistakes and find a way to live comfortably with the results. I finally looked in the mirror and owned that I had been in church for years listening to great preachers dissect the Word of God and hearing the Word from a victim's position rather than a victor's posture. We have all been down dark roads and lonely streets, but it is important to recognize that God uses every daunting midnight experience to propel you forward. The key is knowing that the velocity of your forward motion depends on the state of your mind, and that you should embrace God's Word concerning you and step out on faith daily. "Faithing it" until you see God's Word manifested not only takes time, but also requires self-confidence and commitment to God. Reprioritizing your healthy life over your sick dis-EASED thoughts and behaviors requires courage. So many times, we imagine ourselves sleeping with the enemy, but in fact the INNER ME can be our worst enemy.

Until This August

I never fully connected the dots from my childhood to my adult life, because I lacked the tools to recognize my internal breakdown. Suddenly, however, the lights came on, and I could emotionally digest what happened to me. It was as though the shade that once had dimmed the room was now lifted, and I could see clearly. This clarity of thought emerged when I began speaking my truth regardless of how it impacted others. Until that moment, I had been more focused on others' impressions and interpretations rather than unapologetically giving them my best self with the option to take it or leave it. I started acknowledging my disappointments and embracing my mistakes, and suddenly, I felt an awakening within. I like to call this my personal and intimate deliverance....

Truth requires courage not only to speak it, but to walk in it and to walk it out. Truth demands the courage to embrace it when it is unpopular, unattractive, disheartening, and hard to digest. Sometimes, the anticipation of what lies on the other side of truth is more overwhelming than facing truth itself. The truth is I've been married twice, and both marriages failed. Neither of the men to whom I chose to give myself could have loved me the way that I needed to be loved, because what I needed was a true and honest love of myself. My choice to end those relationships marked the choice to free myself and those around me from emotional commitments that would never be fulfilled. The truth is I accepted that we brought out the worst in each other rather than the best, and that it's dangerous to live in a place of expectation when the ground can't yield a fruitful harvest.

My second marriage had the potential to be great, but it lacked truth, trust, and transparency. It lacked the kind of truth that makes you vulnerable, causing you to reveal secrets, trust blindly, and frees you to resist wrong for the sake of your integrity, character and the covenant we made to God and each other. This Truth motivates me to seek the fully productive and healthy life that I know is destined for me. This Truth cannot fully manifest and germinate within me if pain and frustration are fighting to incarcerate me at all points—pain only smothers the growth of my organic self.

The Gathering

While on life's journey, I have picked up various habits, attitudes, opinions, and convictions from my experiences. I gathered so much baggage of this nature that I didn't have a good idea of my own principles—I had no idea that I was weighed down with the pressure of living up to the expectations of others. I had learned to mask a vital piece of myself. I know today what I didn't know then—*It had to happen in that way.* The remnants of the devastation and disappointment after the smoke cleared forced me to undertake a necessary emotional and vital self-cleansing. I re-evaluated everything I could recall about all of my relationships: my words, my intentions, my mistakes, my baggage, my brokenness, my expectations, and, most of all, my willingness to continue and complete the cycle of folly and foolishness while being devalued and devaluing myself, mistreating myself by co-signing with silence, all while appearing to be valiant. I woke up slowly one Saturday morning and realized that I didn't have to accept the exceptions as the standard. Mediocrity had never been my companion, and I sent her packing that day.

My old, vibrant self was creeping back on the scene. If you know me, you're likely saying, "Oh, no!" My old self was hiding. She had retreated to keep the peace, but on that day, the covers came off. I had dimmed my light and turned down opportunities while waiting for those attached to me to come up to speed. The fearless one was back and grew stronger with each passing day! I suddenly recognized the contents of the bag that I had securely carried with style and function. It took weeks of long hours and a roller coaster of emotions to sort through the contents of the bag: rejection, anger, resentment, and disrespect. During this time of personal questions and answers, my biggest acknowledgement was that my boundaries were blurred because I had stopped honoring myself.

Therefore, since we are surrounded by such a huge

crowd of witnesses to the life of faith, let us strip off every weight that slows us down, especially the sin that so easily trips us up. And let us run with endurance the race God has set before us.

— Hebrews 12: 1 (NIV)

DIARY ENTRY

October 18, 2015 — Consider Us!

I put my baby to bed, and then walked down the hallway into the walk-in closet in my bedroom. I quietly closed the door behind me. I could hear the sound of the television, but I knew that it wasn't loud enough to drown out my cries. I fell to the floor and buried my face in a bag of clothes that I was prepared to donate, and I cried like a baby. I cried until there were no more tears, and then I sobbed until I felt foolish. I had turned the light off so that, if someone came looking for me, I could say that I was praying. These prayers weren't articulate. I merely rocked back and forth in the closet, trying not to think mean thoughts while raging inside, begging God to come and see about me. *How did I get here?* I kicked over shoe boxes and pulled the clothes from the hangers in frustration. *Ugh… I have everything and nothing. This just doesn't add up.*

That night it was about food—fried chicken to be exact. Last month, he had told me that he had been spoiled before he got married, and that no woman of his would ever feed him fried chicken from Bojangles. I said, "Sorry that I insulted you—feed it to Spanky, our dog. He would appreciate it." But that Sunday, he went and picked up Bojangles—but it was just enough for him, and he didn't consider his family. When I mentioned that it would have been nice to know that he had considered his family, too, he emerged from his seat and charged at me across the room, telling me that I was to blame for his inconsideration. *Yo, everything around here gets twisted. I'd be wrong if I capped him in his sleep. Nah, I need to choke this mean joker!*

Strong and wrong!

Apologies, Forgiveness, and Reconciliation

It takes time to purge oneself emotionally—especially when the layers are dense, and the precepts are cemented into the fabric of who you have become. *How did I get here? Was I asleep? Did I bump my head? Would someone pinch me and tell me that I was dreaming?* My reality was shameful, and I owed God, myself, and some people around me an apology for straying this far from the course. I needed to forgive myself and the others who had mishandled me for their own gain, and most of all, I needed to know the power of reconciliation.

I reconcile Notional Amounts, Material Terms, and Derivative Transactions all day at work using the proper tools, and I knew that I had to reconcile with myself and be reconciled back to God using the tool of the Word of God. The Word of God is recorded for our living, and

I acknowledged I needed to sincerely know the Word and to apply it to my life in an effort to navigate this process. This reconciliation wasn't about reciting the Sinner's Prayer; instead, it was about believing that what God said in His Word about me was Truth.

I grew up believing that forgiveness and reconciliation were synonymous, but it wasn't until my awakening, my soul's breaking and repair, that I accepted forgiveness and absolution were dissimilar from reconciliation. When there is offense, forgiveness is more powerful than reconciliation. Reconciliation should be initiated by the offender, and should be considered by the offended—it is a voluntary agreement between two parties to mend fences without the mandate of forgiveness. Reconciliation doesn't mean that things return to the way they were before, because if they were good before, the warring parties wouldn't need to reconcile. Instead, reconciliation means both parties have agreed to move forward with the agreement of new boundaries.

When I truly forgive, it releases me to receive loving and

genuine opportunities that are blocked when I tightly clutch onto hurt, frustration, and disappointment. When I forgave me, I discharged the shame that I had carried for so long. When I forgave me, I slowly dismantled the mountainous years of emotional guilt that seemed insurmountable to conquer. When I forgave me, I chose to give me the opportunity to be free and to walk in a liberty that I had never sincerely known, and I chose to bid fare-thee-well to the weights that had so easily beset me. Self-forgiveness is imperative to your growth. It can hurt when you dare to believe that you are worthy! Changing your mind about *you* and changing the stories that you tell yourself about you is disruptive to your normal pattern. Making the choice to accept that you are uniquely crafted by the Potter, coupled with harsh revelations about your past and the unfathomable truth of the present, can emotionally hurt. You must be willing to examine the underlying circumstances eye-to-eye and must commit to confronting the undeniable and unshakable truth. A portion of my truth was that I didn't choose what I got—I was living out the results of someone else's choices. However, it was up to me, with the help of God the Father, to make good with the remnant. I forgave the men whom I had trusted for betraying me, violating me, and disrespecting me while mishandling God's gift, and this ultimately woke me up to my truth. I forgave them because they didn't have the capacity to do better at the time, or to grasp the depth of their actions. I forgave them because I was mature enough to acknowledge that ignorance is bliss in every situation.

Once I forgave myself, I asked God to forgive me. I asked him to forgive me for allowing my brokenness to lead and drive me into gray and shady places after I had told Him, "I trust you." Father, forgive me for not totally letting you be my compass when I am unsure. Forgive me for allowing my hopes for others to scream louder than your voice during times of uncertainty. Forgive me for turning my back on my untapped potential because I thought I was "ordinary." Forgive me for not totally surrendering every piece of myself to you.

Past failures and losses can entrap you, and can deny you the freedom to enjoy your present and your future.

Brothers and sisters, I do not consider myself yet to have taken hold of it. But one thing I do: Forgetting what is behind and straining toward what is ahead, [14] I press on toward the goal to win the prize for which God has called me heavenward in Christ Jesus. [15] All of us, then, who are mature should take such a view of things. And if on some point you think differently, that too God will make clear to you. -Philippians 3:13-15 (NIV)

Laughable Indignation

__Laughable:__ Causing laughter; funny; amusing; ludicrous
__Indignation:__ Strong displeasure at something considered un-
just, offensive, insulting, or base; righteous anger.

I believe that with truth, forgiveness, and reconciliation comes a level of unadulterated revelation and a stronger understanding of the things that once "appeared" to be hidden. When the scales fell from my eyes, my comprehensive understanding opened, and things with which I had once reasoned and mentally labored, I found myself accepting for what they were. I was emerging from the blind spot.

One morning, I laughed hysterically to keep from crying—the indignation aimed at me by someone else had left me flabbergasted. I laugh with most people, hug lots of people, and genuinely enjoy serving others. I love deeply and intensely; therefore, when I'm hurt, it feels equally as deep and intense. I appreciate palpable, honest, and vulnerable conversation which reveal hearts and raw emotions. I'm attracted to information, data, and facts, so learning and trying new things is intriguing to me. That morning, I laughed until I could no longer laugh, and then I began to shake my head and stare off into space. I had recalculated the known offenses committed against me and my marriage while I received pep talks about being a team player. Hooking up with the home health aide, sleeping with customers, inappropriate remarks made to the neighbor about her body parts, inviting my friend on a double date, with your friend who sat at my kitchen table and your side chick while I stayed home, hooking up with the Pastor's wife... What else could I do but laugh to keep from finding a gun and using it to turn someone's lights out?

I was hurting deeply and intensely, and then, to add insult to injury, the place where I worshipped, where I stood on the front lines fighting and working, did nothing to stand up for me. I wasn't looking for a pity party or a payday from the church but, no one offered a hug, a bag of groceries or a call to ask, "How are you?". Feeling rejected and isolated trying to comprehend how they same people that would call you when they needed you but, overlook you when you truly needed them, instead, they turned away, acted as if it were *my* issue, and they knew nothing about it. The level of cowardice on display each Sunday sickened me. Church used to be a hospital where the sick and heavy-laden came to be delivered, refreshed, encouraged, and renewed, but today it resembles a place where some go to have their agenda served first before they can minister to you. I'm a soul, too. I matter, I hurt, and I, too, have value. Knowing what was staring me in the eye, my church's leadership could have at least offered a hug. Instead, they responded with, "I didn't know." Oh, you knew!

My bitter indignation and frustration were real. I was upset that I was upset, and I was annoyed that I was disgruntled. I was hysterical, because I would never consciously treat people the way in which I had been handled. I am the friend who stands with you when others have embarrassed you, and when you have detoured long before you reach the finish line. I ride with you. After all that I had endured, I acknowledged that I needed a God-encounter on another level to bring me through my pain. People had disappointed me, and sadly, I couldn't bring myself to raise my expectations of them. I needed God to immediately lift my burden. I was enraged with those around me who lied to me and smiled with me—I looked people in the face and dared them to say something to me, because if they did, they were going to get a piece of my mind. It was as though a violent gangster had moved into my body and was waging war with those who had wronged me.

Who was this infuriated woman?

I was looking for a glimmer of hope, but first I had to dig deeper within to embrace the truth about the God of my salvation. The God about whom I had ministered and sang to others could help me, save me, and bring me out on the winning side. It was imperative that I return to the Father, because he didn't desert me—rather, I had turned my back on Him while looking for answers that could only be found in Him. Yes—I needed to make a U-Turn! It was deliverance time. Everything I had smothered and suppressed had risen to the surface, and I needed to deal with it. I took myself back to the same altar to which I had ushered so many others in times past. I no longer needed an outer court experience— this indignation needed the Holy of Holies.

PRINCIPLE: Just because people show up, doesn't mean they're present.

Beautiful Volcano

He said, "I see why them niggas be knockin' women out, you betta be lucky I'm saved"!

My friend's Nigerian Uncle starts most of his philosophical commentary with these two words, "In life..." We tend to laugh at how the gentle giant starts his sentence but have learned over time to listen closely to the wisdom which follows his famous two words. I'll add to his familiar phrase by saying, "In life everything has a beginning and an ending but you have the authority to impact the middle".

It was the evening of Friday, August 28, 2015, we were driving home from a church service where we were celebrating Founder's week (church anniversary), my Pastors wedding anniversary and my Bishop's upcoming birthday. As we were driving home, I'd mentioned that I hadn't eaten all day and had a hunger headache and needed something to eat. I'd ask my husband if he were okay with me stopping at Waffle House to pick up food, he responded, "Sure". As we rode along and recounted the events of the week and evening, I finally pulled into a parking space at Waffle House. I asked, "if he wanted to go inside to dine or order take out, he responded, "This woman doesn't know what she wants to do." Looking confused I asked, "Do you not want anything?" his response, "I want to go home and eat the food in the refrigerator, it's free", actually it wasn't free, I'd purchased it previously. I sat back in my seat and said, "So you don't want anything from here but it didn't seem that way when I mentioned stopping here to get food earlier." His response, "you don't know what you want to do". I placed my wallet on the dashboard, fastened my seatbelt, put the vehicle in reverse and headed to the house. It was a pretty silent ride until he asks, "Why didn't you get anything?" I replied, "It's always complicated and you blamed me for not knowing what I wanted, when I was merely asking you a question, even the simplest things are complicated, I'm good and I'll eat at home".

As we arrive home and I pulled into the parking space he says, "You can go back to the Waffle House and get your food and I'll take the baby inside and put her to bed". I turned to my right and looked at him with a blank stare and asked, "Now what sense does it make for me to go back to a place that I'd just left to get food that I could have gotten when we we're there? You seemed anxious to get home so we're here!" He responds, "Who do you think you're looking at like that, I see why them niggas be knockin' women out, you betta be lucky I'm saved!" My eyeballs bulging from my skull I asked, "Safe or saved?" exited the car and head into the house.

I go into the house and put the baby to bed. Once I'm sure she's asleep I confront him by asking, "Do you think what you said to me outside was right", he responded, "Yes, because of the look you gave me." So, I repeated the question in hopes to get a different answer or perhaps an apology. I stood there and said, "I dare you, you will never work again in any of these here Carolina states, I'll put something on you in prayer that will change everything you put your hands to if you put your hands on me!" I was livid!

I recalled crying hysterically, I boiled in fury, what kind of man says that to his wife, the kind who's more interested in coming home to be alone with his cell phone, where no one can see him sending text messages, that's why you couldn't fellowship after service or wait at Waffle House with me while I picked up food, instead you'd prefer to setup your weekend with friends. The mind games had been played long enough, always flipping stuff on me, reversing what I said, that night it was crystal clear I was connected to someone that had no respect for me as his wife or any other woman. Some of the women that I know who were victims of domestic violence are internally scarred by the punches, kicks and beat downs they received decades ago, long after the scars are healed.

That night I cried endlessly. I cried until my voice was

silent and at times hoarse, my eyes were puffy and I was saddened and exhausted by the constant chaos. Some things you don't say unless you're fighting for your life and threatening to physically harm me because I could see through you was at the bottom of the barrel. I'd grown up in a house where my father would occasionally raise up at my mother but, she would fiercely bring the heat to him. Here I was, hurt on new levels because I was threatened to be physically hit by my husband, the father of my child, nope, I won't join this circle of insanity. I'd been stomaching the constant disrespect and disregard but tonight something shifted within me, I'd reach my breaking point. I was silent for weeks thereafter, I could talk but I didn't want to talk to him. Replaying the events in my head cast me into a severely depressed state and I became withdrawn and aloof, emotionally I toggled between outrage and embarrassment. Two weeks following the shady debacle, he came home and cooked dinner, and would alert me to when dinner was ready. Sometimes, I ate, other times I didn't, I couldn't be bothered to eat food from or with someone that refused to apologize for his comments.

Saturday, August 29, 2015, I received a phone call from one of the leaders at my church informing me that my Bishop died tragically. I was shocked, scared, unsettled and confused; I was anything but "ok". After learning some of the facts surrounding my Bishop's death, I sat myself in the gliding rocking chair that I'd purchased to soothe my daughter and rocked myself for hours. I put many miles on the chair, I got up from the chair to attend to my daughter, then I returned to the rocker to further soothe myself. I couldn't stop thinking about how sad my Bishop's family must have felt, or the initial shock and the many unanswered questions they must've exchanged amongst themselves. When I couldn't rock myself in the rocking chair, I sat still on the ottoman in the bathroom staring into space, thinking what just happened.

This was truly a hard time for me, I constantly thought of the first family and couldn't imagine the deep pains they were feeling, I remembered the faithful church congregants, his sons and daughters in ministry, his mom and siblings, his peers which returned home only hours ago after celebrating with him. This loss was enormous and was going to hit hard, I constantly remembered his smile and his words from the night before. I thought to myself, death is deafening, nippy and it can frustrate you with its unnerving finality; you cannot return from death, you can only face the void.

I selfishly thought about myself and what his passing meant for me. Only 6 months earlier I sat in his office trying to sort through the bumps and potholes I was facing in my own life. I vividly remember him searching for a pencil and pad to take notes. Bishop calculated the number of months between the wedding ceremony, the age of my daughter and number of times we'd separated in under three years. Bishop said, "You've been through too much in a short period of time and there's no resolution to any of the issues. Who've you been talking too, where is your support system?" All I could do was weep… this was too much for one person to shoulder!

The final weekend of August 2015 was detrimental to my mental health. Friday I was threatened to be physically harmed and with no apology in sight or attempt to heal what was broken. Saturday my Bishop suddenly passed away leaving a hole in our hearts. Many things died that weekend; my hope for my marriage was dying and my Pastor was gone, a little piece of me died that weekend. Externally I smiled but internally I was dead, brain dead and mentally depleted from the constant noise.

After weeks of prayer and fasting I tried to mentally recalibrate but I just couldn't lock in. I was sad, pitiful and heartbroken. My husband had come to me one evening with an observation, he said, "You grieved more over Bishop than my mother when she died". I took a deep breath, paused then said, "you don't know how I grieved for your mom, you'd left me and the baby and weren't here?" There goes the mind game again, the crafty and cunning ability to turn everything on others, be accountable for your actions! I wasn't grieving for any person, I was grieving the death of my marriage.

Friday, August 29th was the night my heart ruptured like a climatic volcano. Deep within my core the chaos and confusion were diverging, tossing me in many directions from one common point, my heart, my love, and my truth. The rumbling that took place in the innermost parts of me were due to unrest, nothing seemed to bring me solace.

My mind constantly replayed the events of that weekend. The hot resentment which boiled within began to pour over my body repeatedly, I was frightened, and I'd held so much inside waiting for respect and truth to show itself, it's as though my patience had ended. The trauma to my mind and spirit married to the stress in my body was too much, I exploded emotionally - I couldn't take it anymore. I'm sorry he took my patience, consistency and posture as a weakness. Every woman isn't rolling her neck and raising her voice and eyebrows to express herself. I sing loud but speak low when facing confrontation at home.

The volcano is beautiful. The internal aggravation that was constantly percolating inside erupted, causing the pain to shoot up and spill out, thus recreating its shape and reinforcing the outer walls. It was as though I'd been put on the Potter's wheel, God saw the vessel was marred in His hands and made me again.

And the vessel that he made of clay was marred in the hand of the potter: so he made it again another vessel, as seemed good to the potter to make it.

– Jeremiah 18:4 (KJV)

I wanted the weekend to be different, I didn't want my Bishop to die because we needed him and, I didn't want my marriage to die because my daughter and I needed my husband. I knew we were in the final leg of the race, the final baton was passed, there were no more hurdles to cross, just the final stretch to the finish line. This would be the final August the volcano was nudged to the point of eruption. The final time I'd be told I was the lucky benefactor of someone's salvation, I was safe in the arms of Jesus and he'd lifted a standard against the enemy; finally, I could see the weapon was formed, but didn't prosper against me.

By August 2016 I was divorced. Look at the beautifully handcrafted and textured volcano, full of personality re-shaped and resized and prepared for what's next. I was no longer being stirred within by the constant conflict; instead I'm waiting with expectation for what God is go-ing to do.

In life things aren't always as they appear. When choosing to be in relationship with others after ex-periencing divorce, don't allow physical appear-ance or money to draw you into the person. Join yourself to someone with good character that will run to you and not away from you during hardship.

~ Gbeye Fawehinmi

Encounter

Wednesday, January 13, 2016, I mounted the pulpit on assignment. My focus was laser-straight—I would deliver a Word that I was sure God had given me for this church. I had to live this Word, digest it, and dare to believe again. During the weeks leading up to this engagement, the enemy had waged war against my daughter, my household, and my body, and was trying desperately to enter my mind. But I was unwilling to give into the negativity that pressed against me. I was determined not to wave the white flag of surrender!

Finally, brethren, whatsoever things are true, whatsoever things are honest, whatsoever things are just, whatsoever things are pure, whatsoever things are lovely, whatsoever things are of good report; if there be any virtue, and if there be any praise, think on these things. -Philippians 4: 8 (KJV)

That night, my text was from the gospel of St. Mark 5: 23–34, and the mnemonic device was "When Believing Hurts." Can you imagine Jesus and Jairus walking together, side-by-side, and how optimistic Jairus must have felt discovering the healing power that lived in Jesus, and that it would soon address his daughter's needs? If I were Jairus walking with Jesus, I would have been happier than a kid in a toy store knowing that I was next in line, and that it was *my* time to receive the goodies. Then, suddenly, you find yourself stopped by someone who has allowed their hungry faith to move them out of a familiar yet uncomfortable place to interrupt the pattern of complacency in their life.

When faith is alive, it moves and breathes. It carries you through transition. Faith is present when you stand victoriously on the mountain, and it motivates you when you're hunkered down in the dark valley. The confidence of faith challenges our complacency and our willingness to sit in dry places, desperately trying to embrace progress while lacking the vulnerability to believe again. The woman with the Issue of Blood kissed mediocrity good-bye when she decided to get up from the place that had a constant stench and decided to believe in God for more. In the weeks leading up to this assignment, God petitioned me, "What will you believe me to do?"

This message hit home. Here was Jairus, walking alongside Jesus while the crowds were growing around them, and he assumed that *he* was next. There was a woman in transit who was determined to have an encounter with Jesus while Jairus casually walked with Him. She bumped against Jesus due to the size of the growing crowd, and in doing so, she snuffed out Jairus's spot in line and stole the "next" position.

The unnamed woman pushed through the growing crowd because she was desperate and thirsty, in need of change and exhausted with her norm—she wanted an encounter, and she wanted to know personally how healing and wholeness felt. I can imagine that she was determined to get to Jesus and refused to be deterred or stopped along the way because of what she believed for herself. She knew that her future was bigger than what she presently faced. We occasionally take the Jairus stroll, claiming to walk alongside the Savior, yet we do not truly understand the magnitude of the power contained within Him. Lightly brushing up beside Him when trouble hits, praying occasionally, and fasting when conveniently reminded, failing to reach beyond boundaries that make us uncomfortable—but this woman wanted a personal encounter.

I was like the unnamed woman in so many ways. I needed a life-changing encounter with God. In order for that to happen, I had to unfasten myself from bitter indignation and desperately pursue the healing that I so deeply needed. Untying myself meant I had to make myself uncomfortable with the private pain with which I had become so familiar, and walk toward the God of my salvation.

When I touched Him, the virtue of God transformed me immediately. His touch revealed the layers of deception—everything dark was brightened, hidden things were revealed, and transparency became the gauge and thermometer for my healing and deliverance.

PRINCIPLE: Each encounter needs vulnerability to achieve a materialized corrective action.

What I Know Today

Nothing just happens. There are no wasted experiences, unnecessary tears, or impossible situations. There is such a thing as an avoidable situation. If God allows you to collide with devastation to teach or mature you and it's the cause of your perception change, you can trust it's working for your good and His glory. Perhaps you had to face the humiliation of the abuse you hid, or you have lived with the pain of rejection while learning to accept the fate of your reality. Today, I know that there is an opportunity to grow in and through each experience. Your perception of yourself will determine how you posture yourself—as victim or victor. What I know today is that no matter how many people are standing on the sidelines of your life, they don't have the right to navigate the storm with which you've collided.

I have opinionated friends and family members, and I've walked on roads and sat at tables they haven't. I didn't agree with the decisions they made for their lives, so I gave them the side eye, thinking, *how can you see so clearly for me, yet your path is full of gaping holes and dysfunctions you don't have the courage to correct?* I didn't think I was better than they were, but I knew that I was bolder, risky, outspoken, and unashamed; I knew that I was unapologetic about my opinions, convictions, and passions, and what I would and would not accept. I was a superhero within, and I could do anything I put my mind to do. I wasn't hiding behind my insecurities to make others feel better about themselves. It's true you can have success in one area of your life and be severely damaged in another. One day while sharing a lunch hour with a colleague and sister-friend Kiyoko, she encouraged me after I shared my story, and we laughed at my unbelievable made-for-TV life story with three powerful words: "Keep choosing you!" As I began to process these words, I was taken aback. She then followed up by saying, "I'm not saying to be selfish, but I am saying that you should always consider yourself first. Only then will you be healthy enough to safely choose for someone else." I hit the jackpot that day—this woman has laughed with me at lunch and rolled her eyes in anger toward me in the boardroom, but that day she helped the lights shine a little brighter for me.

What I know today is that much healing and deliverance can manifest in the uncultivated seasons of your life. I stepped down from a leadership position in my church because I needed to focus on me and my family. While it was the best decision, I made it so I could regroup, refocus and redefine myself. I needed the wilderness so that God could address and heal my hurts, pains, and disappointments. I needed God to restore my vision, because even I had recognized that my sight was limited due to the unending emotional turmoil that I faced, I needed the wilderness so that I could mend. In the wilderness, God reinforced His love for me, gave me an understanding of this August season, and delivered me from my indignation. I needed the wilderness so that I could see, feel and hope again. I had become hardened and numb by the storm, and I traded the best part of my prayer life for fussing and damning. I was alive, but I wasn't living. The wilderness, although dark and lonely, was sobering and peaceful; here is where I faced my depression and sadness. I fought and prevailed against the darkness, climbing to a place that was emotionally healthy and hopeful. One thing I came to understand while facing my conflict was when you love someone you will endure pain, but once you start loving yourself, you reject pain and put it on notice-you cannot keep coming back here! Pain today builds strength for tomorrow but the redundancy of trauma to the same place creates callousness.

What I know today is that some of us never truly allow God to interfere or intervene until we've been emotionally hog tied and are forced to a halt. We keep God at church until we need to bring Him home. It is only when our will breaks that we allow the God of our salvation to penetrate our broken hearts, steady our minds, and handle those situations that have handled us. We have mastered lifting our hands and praising the Lord, but it takes time to master the posture of surrender and to relinquish all things to God. We talk about it, think about it, pray and worry about it, and handle it until we're pushed into a corner and slammed to the ground because it's handling us. We allow God to lead us only when we feel exhausted and depleted. It is then that we learn that His strength is made perfect in our weakness.

Today, I know that I am a product of my environment—good, bad, or indifferent. My parents grew up in a time of racism and segregation, when you didn't and couldn't say much. Instead, they took what they were given and made the best of it. I've seen them humble themselves and accept what they are given rather than speak up and give voice to their feelings and thoughts. I'm the opposite of my parents—if I take issue with my circumstances, I start asking questions as I process what's in front of me. Today, I am not ashamed of who I am, what I've faced, or what I've become, because I am not defined by my mistakes or the poor decisions of my past.

Don't be complicit in the attempted downgrade. You can safely admit when someone is not enough for you, in doing so you acknowledge you deserve more than that particular individual can give. Consider your self-awareness and oneness with God as a global positioning system "GPS" which brings you to only emotionally healthy destinations. Possess enough strength as the keeper of your heart and life to not make yourself the breeding ground for others insecurities, lies and falsehood. Love yourself enough to let your truth be realized from afar, and reject the notion that you are not ready for what's next when it comes wrapped in deceit and camouflaged as truth.

I will praise thee; for I am fearfully and wonderfully made: marvellous are thy works; and that my soul knoweth right well. -Psalms 139: 14 (KJV)

And we know that all things work together for good to them that love God, to them who are the called according to his purpose. Romans 8: 28 (KJV)

What I know today is that some of my biggest fears were realized during this August season. I didn't die from facing them, and neither did they kill me. Yes—they were monstrosities from afar, but the closer I came to facing them, the more clearly, I could see God slaying the giants and helping me through these difficult times. Everything is not perfect, neither am I satisfied with every outcome, but God has graced me with time and discernment, and is developing me for what His plans. I fully understand that man will never have God's glory. God will shut the mouths of the nay-sayers, condemn every tongue that rises against you in judgment, and exalt you in due season.

I know that God has great plans for me. It takes courage and a touch of untethered greatness to overcome the abuse, misfortune, and disappointment that I have experienced. For some, it may take a lifetime to shed the weights of shame and condemnation, because these individuals are more concerned with keeping up appearances than with embracing their fears and facing the fire. Perhaps the fire you so fiercely resist is the fire you need to refine and increase your self-worth. Then there are others may harbor bitterness for a lifetime, waiting for apologies that never come, and waiting to gain closure from conversations that will never be scheduled.

What I know today is that I don't need man—I don't need the arms of flesh to fight, defend, claim, or stand up for me. In this August season, I wanted my husband to fight for his family; I wanted the church leadership to stand up for me when I felt ambushed and mishandled; I even wanted my boss to fight for me when others misunderstood my expressions. I've had many private moments with my 10-year-old self, but on that day, I spoke with my adult self, and proclaimed, "God is fighting for you, and has predetermined what your victory looks like." As a mature and better-informed woman, I know that some of the men with whom I connected deeply were broken and needed rescue from their own giants. Our self-serving broken parts are what attracted us to each other and bonded us emotionally.

I know today is that God loves me, and that nothing just happens. I was fortunate to have loving parents who made me wonder if we were wealthier than we were and not because of materialistic things but because of their love and commitment to me. I never went without necessities or missed meals, and I never intimately knew neglect. My parents were and still are my greatest teachers and encouragers.

And they overcame Him by the blood of the Lamb, and by the word of their testimony; and they loved not their lives unto the death. -Revelation 12: 11 (KJV)

DIARY ENTRY

It's All Over, Saturday, June 16, 2018

These last two months have been filled with a myriad of emotions and revelations. I've been exhausted by cumbersome conversations about nothingness, confused by stubbornness, and overwhelmed by ignorance, and I've questioned myself. *Am I doing the right thing? Am I being petty? Am I muddying the waters? Am I going overboard?* And of course, the biggest question of all—*Am I operating from a place of fear?*

It is true that hurt people damage other people. I don't want to be the one inflicting wounds on others, and I don't want to leave them to ask and answer hard questions regarding the devastation that I ushered into their lives. I simply love life and God too much to consciously be that person. About those bugs… I've

listened to the stories that others have told about boda-
cious water bugs. I've heard their screams, and I've
watched them scamper down hallways trying to avoid
collisions with the vermin. All the while, for the three
weeks of commotion going on around me, God put me
on a consecration, and He protected me from the normal course of business when the water bugs would stop
me in my tracks and warn me of an upcoming attack.
This time, God strategically changed my desire to take a
familiar route in the natural world, which was indicative
of what He was doing in the spiritual realm, as well. I
chuckled with assurance when God revealed that He was
bringing me out of the blind spot! No longer did I need
to seek control—I was promoted to being in charge,
simply because I surrendered to God and recognized
that He is fighting for me.

The LORD will fight for you; you need only to be
still. -Exodus 14: 14 (NIV)

Yesterday morning, while lying in bed, I awoke to an un-
usual tingling sensation that covered my body from head

to toe. When my feet hit the floor, I immediately said, "Thank you, Lord," and then I looked around me to ensure that everything was all right. At first, I rebuked the stress from my body. As I stilled myself and acknowledged that the Lord was covering me with His blood, I hushed my mouth and settled my spirit to watch Him work on my behalf. Fighting for yourself doesn't mean that you must use nasty words or be mean, but that you must stand in your truth. You must take a position.

I'm out of the blind spot. To God be the Glory!

The Journal

I've been journaling for as long as I can remember—
Sunday, June 7, 1987 was my first journal entry. I've
kept journals in my purse, near my bed, or in a secret
location so that others couldn't easily access them. The
lined pages of these journals were a safe place for me to
share my truth, my stories, my experiences, my hurts,
my expectations and aspirations—the journal was a
window into my world. For a season, I stopped journaling, because I couldn't trust that my secrets would
be honored if discovered. I was unsure how I could rationalize the confusion that lined the pages, so I simply
put away the tools that had so often rescued me from
depression or delirium. During this season, I learned
how to keep notes within myself—I became the curved
strokes on the page; I was the words and the lines on
the pages; I embodied the memories and events; the
pages were me, slowing turning while life filled them

with poignant experiences and vivid emotions, at times colorful and at times colorless. The more that I reviewed and relived the events inside me, the deeper they dug into my soul. This prompted me to capture the timely and systematic events below, as these events were pivotal to my growth, maturity, and deliverance. I am a living letter and description of God's Mercy, Grace, and Handiwork—a workman who need not be ashamed.

AUGUST 2013 / AUGUST 2014 / AUGUST 2015 / AUGUST 2016

1st ~ The call; making dinner plans without me. (08/1/2014)

2nd ~ It's my requirement, but I'm afraid to attend the Farewell, because it's also a meet and greet. (01/2/2015)

3rd ~ You can run, but you can't hide; who are you? (Vehicles); the Pastor's wife (09/3/2017); the sponsor (05/3/2018)

4th ~ Queens, New York with the Prophet A.C., and it came to pass (02/4/2015)

5th ~ Denied; dead on arrival; water bugs; "Remembering Our Legacy" (08/5/2017)

6th ~ Untying; in relationship (are YOU seeing anyone?) (08/6/2013); packing and unpacking (1st displacement 12/6/2013); water bugs in boot camp (08/6/2014)

7th ~ Mirena, I can't find you; It ain't mine, it's the one beating your guts! (08/7/2015); back in the saddle; with sympathies, you're making a bad decision (05/7/2015)

8th ~ Stressed from the inside out (12/8/2014)

9th - 11th ~ Surfside, SC repairing the breach (4/9-

11/2015)

12th ~ After counseling; "Knock Knock, who is there?" (Premier's Joy, 12/12/2013); untied divorce (08/12/2016)

13th ~ Thirteen is not a lucky number, but it reveals truth; the plant needs sunlight but the sun (ME) moved 08/13/2016)

14th ~ Tied (04/14/2012); whole or term life – you get nothing! (2014)

15th ~ Stop contacting me, delete my number Dorsey (05/15/2013); some love to prey – M. Papo (10/15/2016)

16th ~ The wind must have blown your business card here Mr. Policeman (07/16/2016)

17th ~ By the fall of the year, the last 10 months will make sense (07/17/2014 Prophet A.C.)

18th ~ Cussed me because of pain and confusion (12/18/2014); the day the stars aligned and the "weights" moved (The shift - Prophet A.C. 08/18/2014 and 08/18/2016); Rule 60 Motion (09/18/2017)

19th ~ Las Vegas water bugs (04/19/2012)

20th ~ 911; embrace me but DO NOT PUT YOUR HANDS-ON ME! (01/20/2013); the birthing, or girl meets world (08/20/2013); the cold disconnect and the funeral (12/20/2015); Bi-Lo meeting in the dark (01/20/2016); the underground reveals truth (05/20/2016); packing… no, unpacking (3rd displacement 03/20/2016); water bugs in the no-fly zone – CAAC (09/20/2017)

21th ~ Thanksgiving, run to her (11/21/2013)

22nd ~ Happy birthday to me!

23rd ~ Fighting for self (08/**23**/2013); Dream-Plants offer provision for life and knowledge (03/**23**/2014); five in planter fatigues; invitation to double date with a friend

– Jazz band 3rd Saturday – Vaps (08/23/2014)

24th Houges' prophetic dream; check your trash cans for recycling (06/24/2014); packing and unpacking (2nd displace-ment 12/24/2014); the truth keeps finding me 2 doors down (09/24/2017)

25th ~ We moved! Out with the old and into the new (08/25/2016)

26th ~ She left and we didn't get to say good-bye (12/26/2014)

27th ~ The worst day ever (2014), The meeting with Bishop and Pastor C.L. (3/27/2015)

28th ~ I cut my eye about

the Waffle House – see how people get knocked out (08/28/2015); THIS IS NOT NORMAL! In charge vs. in control (08/28/2017); over the hurdle, overnight (09/28/2017)

29th ~ It's not mine (12/29/2012); Bishop passed away – death is deafening (08/29/2015)

30th ~ Can't hold it any longer (house guest & celebration) 08/30/2014

31st ~ Messenger with friends (07/31/2014); I'm no longer debating about the nights out (09/31/2014); the flying laundry basket, I finally surrendered, take what you want. (01/31/2016)

Counseling Resources

Ru'ahh, the Wind, the Breath, and the Spirit of God,

Pastoral Counseling c/o TRS Professional Suites

40 Exchange Place, 3rd floor

New York, NY 10005

Office: 212-685-2848

Mobile: 646-705-6194

Guide to Introspection

Before you close this book please take a moment to explore the questions below. Remember that because an incident is in the past, that doesn't mean you've processed the trauma. We often hold others responsible for our pain but, the key to promoting healthy emotional growth is to look inward and offer your broken self, honest insight into what carried you to this place.

1. What themes keep repeating themselves in my life and how can I break the cycle?

_____

_____

_____

_____

2. Am I holding onto shame and disappointment?

_____

_____

_____

_____

3. Have I forgiven the individual(s) that hurt me?

_____

_____

_____

_____

4. Do I truly want to move forward?

_____

_____

_____

_____

5. What does God say about me?

_____

_____

_____

_____

6. Can I endure the negative feelings that may arise because of my decision to work on me?

_____

_____

_____

_____

If feelings of regret and anger surfaced while you combed through your mind examining your life experiences, go back and read the prayer at the beginning of the book. You're in a good place for God to deliver you, deep spiritual wounds are real and should not be diminished or overlooked. You cannot simply get over them you must work through them. Getting over is what you've done for far too long, some wounds last decades because we are unwilling to commit to treatment. Yes, there are times when God will perform a miracle in our lives and heal us immediately of the pain and there are times when we have to go through the process.

Make time to sit quietly and love on yourself, personally celebrate your accomplishments, we often deny ourselves true intimacy but expect it from others. Private intimacy with self will help you overcome the disappointment of others if they never celebrate you publicly. Know and believe what God has said about you. Don't live too long in the low moments, instead let them propel you to your next peak.

Here's your self-work, daily, take a moment to meditate on the scriptures and affirmations below to build your self-esteem and know what God's intentions are for your life, and you will see yourself budding and transforming into a beautiful flower.

Cleanse the wound

Pray: We must earnestly come to God in faith asking Him to cleanse us and trust that He will make us whole.

- ***If we confess our sins, He is faithful and just to forgive us our sins, and to cleanse us from all unrighteousness. - 1 John 1:9 (KJV)***

Bandage the wound

Protect: We must consistently protect our mind by renewing it daily with the Word of God.

- ***And be not conformed to this world: but be ye transformed by the renewing of your mind, that ye may prove what is that good,***

and acceptable, and perfect, will of God. –
Romans 12:2 (KJV)

Observe the wound

Watch: Spiritual wounds are no different than physical injuries, they require special attention to heal properly. We must monitor our company and our conversation, infection spreads quickly and the enemy wants you to dwell on the injustice but you have the authority to shut him down.

- *Be sober, be vigilant; because your adversary the devil walketh about as a roaring lion, seeking whom he may devour. - 1 Peter 5:8 (KJV)*

Emotional Healing Scriptures

Sin, abuse, neglect, rejection, betrayal...all cause great emotional and spiritual pain that hurt just as physical pain does. God, our Great Physician can completely heal our broken hearts and bind our wounds, healing and making us whole. Spiritual and emotional healing is often a process with steps that we need to put action behind.

- *A cheerful heart is good medicine, but a crushed spirit dries up the bones. -- Proverbs 17:22 (NIV)*

- *LORD, be gracious to us; we long for you. Be our strength every morning, our salvation in time of distress. -- Isaiah 33:2 (NIV)*

- *Therefore confess your sins to each other and pray for each other so that you may be healed. The prayer of a righteous person is powerful and effective. -- James 5:6 (NIV)*

- *He gives strength to the weary and increases the power of the weak. -- Isaiah 40:29 (NIV)*

- *Hear, Lord, and be merciful to me; Lord, be my help." [11] You turned my wailing into dancing; you removed my sackcloth and clothed me with joy, [12] that my heart may sing your praises and not be silent. Lord my God, I will praise you forever. -- Psalms 30:10-12 (NIV)*

About the Author

Kimberly D. Benn is a native of the Bronx, New York. She was educated in the private Parochial and Catholic schools of the Bronx, New York. She studied under-graduate at IONA College in New Rochelle, NY and graduated with a Bachelor of Science in Humanities. Then upon relocating to Charlotte she obtained a Bachelor of Science in Biblical Studies from Queen City Bible College. Kimberly is the founder of Naomi's Posture, Inc., a women's ministry in Charlotte, North Carolina. The heartbeat of Naomi's Posture is to en-courage and inspire women to stand strong and, hold fast to what God has said about them in spite of life's unexpected interruptions.

Made in the USA
Middletown, DE
04 July 2019